M000297794

THE LAST STRAW

CHANGE YOUR LIFE AND THE PLANET - FOR GOOD

JOYCE KRISTIANSSON

The Last Straw.

Copyright © 2020 by Joyce Kristiansson

All rights reserved. No part of this book may be reproduced or used in any manner without written permission of the copyright owner except for the use of quotations in a book review. For more information, address: joyce@ thelaststrawbook.com.

FIRST EDITION

www.thelaststrawbook.com

ISBN ebook: 978-1-64921-844-5
ISBN paperback: 978-1-64921-845-2

For all the hopeful ones.

And the ones who want to be hopeful.

"It is the last straw that breaks the camel's back."

– **Charles Dickens**

CONTENTS

INTRODUCTION

TEN WEEKS TO BETTER PEOPLE
AND A BETTER PLANET

"Small acts, when multiplied by millions of people,
can transform the world."
– Howard Zinn

What do you feel when you see plastic bags blowing in the wind, caught in trees and fence lines, floating in our waterways? Do you notice?

Is it really our problem as individuals? We didn't allow *our* bags to end up there, and sometimes we have even picked up bags tossed aside by others.

Certainly, the manufacturers that make them and the retailers that provide them have a huge role to play in alleviating the problem.

Oftentimes when we see something that we believe is wrong or that we think we could help with, we want to take action and do something, but it seems impossible. There are just too many obstacles in the way. We don't have enough time, we don't see the impact, we don't know how.

My hope is that if we can get our lives into balance, we can find the time, see the impact, and have the capacity to learn how—and as a result, change our habits in a way that allows us to do better for ourselves and for the environment.

Better habits, better health, better happiness, and better relationships lead to a better environment.

Is it possible that by acting with our collective force as individuals, we can change the supply and demand balance by reducing the use of plastic bags, straws, and similar items?

On the way to becoming the people we are today, our habits were shaped and formed by our experiences, often without us even knowing. Little did we know that some of the experiences that were forming and shaping us were also constraining us. It is only upon self-reflection that we can see how our particular stories unfolded and how the lessons we learned—or thought we learned—along the way informed our current ways of being.

It takes work to unravel the stories we have so carefully knitted together about ourselves—but it's worth it.

After reinforcing the foundations of our daily living—sleep

and play—we can begin to dissect our story and start to act in a way that is more aligned with our true selves. This means spending our time and money more intentionally, serving others, shedding the negative stories we tell ourselves, stretching ourselves, creating mindful habits, making space for what is important to us, and then sharing it in an impactful way.

Letting go of the stories that hold us back can allow us to make space for something better, something that might just surprise us.

These are my stories. I frame these stories as lessons learned because they are the things I determined to be true at that time in my life. They informed my way of thinking and being and seeing the world—some in a good way, some not so much. I had to debunk some of these lessons in order to create the space needed to get to a better place. In that better place we become people and better people create a better planet.

LESSONS LEARNED

It should have been the happiest time of my life. I had a beautiful four-year-old son and one-year-old daughter, my husband and I were working in careers that both challenged us and paid well, we had a live-in au pair to care for our children while we were working, and we owned a home in a beautiful, safe neighborhood in the country.

Instead I was deeply depressed. I went through the motions, did everything that was expected of me, and was desperately tired. Instead of enjoying bath time with my little ones, it was an exercise to get through just so they could go to bed—which meant I could, too. Even my time outdoors, which usually rejuvenated me, was spent sitting in a patio chair staring into space. I was unable to articulate to my husband and those close to me just how unhappy I was. After all, I was living the American dream!

For six months in that state, I plotted how to leave my job. How to walk away from what started out as my dream position with a six-figure income at a Fortune 500 company whose environmental ideals aligned with my own. My self-esteem suffered; what had I done wrong? I always did my best work, but somehow, that wasn't enough. I wasn't just depressed, I was scared. Scared to stay and scared to leave.

I was struggling to mesh my two selves—the one who wanted to be seen as a stay-at-home mom, and the one who wanted to be seen as a working professional. Yet, I couldn't see myself as only a full-time mom, and I couldn't see myself staying in what had become "the daily grind." During those six months, turning it all over and over and over in my mind, I realized that sometimes you have to leave something to build something that allows you to be you (and still make a living!).

I am not the first woman to struggle with this internal conflict. We strive to "have it all" but don't really know how to make that happen. I was determined to have it all, my way. But I had to let go of many of the lessons I had learned along the way and dig deep to rediscover me.

Lesson 1:
It's a Boy's World but Girls Can Find Fun Too

When I graduated from a high school class of fifty-seven students in rural, Southern Illinois, it seemed as though I had two choices in a county with a population of 7,500 people: become a farmer or become a farmer's wife.

The second of four children, my older sister and I shadowed my dad, a part-time farmer and daytime Western Union employee, as much as we were allowed. I vividly remember a time when I was preschool age wanting to be with my dad when he harvested corn on our little eight-acre farm where we lived at that time in Central Illinois. My parents tried to convince me that I wouldn't like it, but I was insistent. It was cold, so my mom bundled me up like a little version of the Michelin Man, and they placed me in the back of the wagon, away from the trajectory of ear corn shot there from the corn picker. It was so cold and very noisy. I quickly found it wasn't what I thought it would be, but I had to wait until my dad reached a stopping point before I could get out. Sometimes, things just aren't what you think they will be.

The highlight of our childhood days was accompanying our

dad to the feed store, dusty and sweet smelling from all the ground feed, and being allowed to get a bottled soda and candy from the old-style vending machines. My dad was raising pigs at the time, and I followed him around doing that as well, muddy and smelly as it was. I am frequently reminded that I said to anyone who was listening, "I'm not going to be a pig woman!"

Then the third child, a boy, arrived. Suddenly, my sister and I were no longer allowed to accompany our dad on his various farm errands; only our little brother accompanied him now. I'm sure that three kids were just too many to haul around, and we couldn't fit in the cab of the old Ford truck anyway. We were also told we couldn't go to the stockyard because of the bad language we might hear—which was apparently okay for the younger ears of our little brother!

That was when I first learned that things were different for boys and girls, and I didn't like it one bit. So I wasn't encouraged to be a farmer—that was for my brother—and I could not see myself as a farmer's wife. From what I saw, the farmer's wife's job was to support the men by cooking and carrying food to them during the long days of planting and harvesting. I know many women, including my mom, who have done just that and enjoyed it, so I am in no way disrespecting that choice. A farming way of life can be a fulfilling partnership and a wonderful way to raise a family. For me, it was a reminder that there were unspoken role expectations that I didn't understand

and that I didn't fit.

The gender role message was reinforced in other ways as well. I missed the bus one morning because I refused to put on the dress my mom had laid out for me. Who can tumble with the boys at recess in a skirt? I remember our Brownies (little Girl Scouts) meetings sitting in the elementary school cafeteria making angels out of cardboard toilet paper dowels, imagining how our Cub Scout counterparts must surely be out hiking in the forest, following stream beds for miles, exploring under every rock and fallen tree. By eighth grade, I had a science teacher who gave us credit for an outdoor education class every summer. He got to go fishing, and we got to traipse around in the woods like Cub Scouts, whether we were boys or girls.

So sometimes we do find a safe spot that lets us just *be*.

Lesson 2:
Zero Money Is Okay with Zero Debt—and a Job

By tenth grade, we had moved closer to my dad's aging parents and now lived on more than 140 beautiful acres of woods with rolling hills and creeks in Southern Illinois. It was wonderful for taking long walks to explore nature, but too remote for much of a teenage social life. After graduation from high school, I went off to college at Southern Illinois University Carbondale, picking a major from my favorite subject, biology.

I had and still have a deep love of science, so biology (with a chemistry minor) was my degree plan, although I had no idea what to do with it. I found some volunteer work that I enjoyed while in college, which landed me in the environmental field, thanks to friends I made there.

After graduation and a summer of work so I would have gas money, I traveled north to Chicago. My aunt and uncle generously opened their home in suburban Chicago to me. I stayed with them until I could save enough money from my new job to get the first and last month's rent and security deposit required to rent an apartment.

I had always thought I was poor—dirt poor—but now I realize I was actually well-off compared to many college graduates today. Between my jobs, short-term loans, and grants, I managed to graduate with zero money, but also zero debt. And I was lucky enough to have a job!

Lesson 3:
Sometimes You Have to Move to the Passing Lane

When I went to Chicago to work with an environmental services contractor, I thought I would stay with that company forever. After three or four years, they transferred me from Chicago to Houston and I was promoted to general manager of their new division where hazardous waste was treated. I worked ninety-hour weeks just for the love of building something new, and I really enjoyed the chemistry and understanding the regulatory classification systems.

Everything changed the day I dared to speak up to management, suggesting that we should not receive a particular waste stream that we were expected to handle; it was lucrative but had a strong acrid odor that caused a lot of problems. That act of speaking up cost me the position. I was demoted; I returned to Chicago briefly until I found a new job at an environmental consulting firm back in humid but sunny Houston. The demotion reminded me that no amount of hard work would be enough to allow me to have a say. I was expected to keep my head down and to stay in my lane. Time to move to the passing lane instead!

Moving from contractor to consultant was a step in the right direction, but I soon realized that there was no career path for me in a consulting firm since I was neither an engineer nor a man. Although I had a female boss, an engineer who was extremely competent and an integral part of the office, she never moved up in the company. If she couldn't do it, what hope did I have?

I knew that to get the next good salary bump, I would need to move from contracting and consulting to an industrial company, so I accepted a position as an environmental supervisor at a crude oil terminal two hours east of Houston in Beaumont, Texas. They paid my moving expenses including $5,000 for "incidentals." I laugh now at how amazed I was. I had never heard of such a thing—money for "incidentals." I learned a lot about the energy business there, thanks to the kindness of the operations manager for whom no question was too dumb.

During this time, my now husband, Lars, and I had started dating and decided to get married. Lars still lived in Houston, and I was lucky to get an opportunity to move back to the Houston area when my company moved its corporate offices from Los Angeles to Sugar Land, a Houston suburb.

So after two years in the Beaumont area, I transferred to the company's re-located corporate office to serve first as the water advisor and then as a shared international environmental advisor. It was some of the most interesting work I have done, including about ten trips to Nicaragua to secure a permit from the environmental ministry for a geothermal project. My son was only about a year old during this project and it hurt my heart to leave him even for a short period of time. He, of course, was totally fine and well cared for by his dad. My daughter was born during my tenure with this company as well. With two little ones at home and the geothermal work that took me to Central America cancelled, it looked more and more like I would be required to travel to Indonesia.

With the work in Indonesia looming, I was concerned about the potential for a long time away from my family. So when I was called by a headhunter about a position as an environmental team leader for a Fortune 500 company with an excellent reputation for environmental stewardship, I was thrilled. I had arrived—or at least I was on my way. Growing up in a small town, the kind that musician John Cougar Mellencamp wrote about, I would have never dreamed that I could work for such a well-known international company. I had hit the big leagues! Although there was some travel with the new job, it was domestic and less frequent. I could enjoy my kids and have a professional life. I was ecstatic to be a part of such a great company.

Lesson 4:
The Boss Can Be More Important than the Job

As they say, people don't leave companies, they leave bosses. And so it was for me. Just as I was hired, the supervisor who hired me was saying farewell and I was introduced to his replacement. Let's just say that when your new boss pulls out his wallet to show you the very worn Bible verse his mother has given him cautioning against anger, it's not a good sign.

I was still not great at company politics, and after about a year it became evident that this was a required skill not listed in the job description. I needed a change. I loved the company and what they were doing and really wanted to stay, so I asked for a transfer to another group where I could apply my skills. My boss denied the transfer request.

That was the last straw.

Less than two years after being recruited for the position, I handed in my resignation. My boss now offered me the transfer but by the time he reconsidered, the wheels had already been set in motion for my next big career move.

I formed a limited liability company (LLC) and was set to go out on my own as a sole proprietor environmental consultant. My kids were now five and two. My son was entering kindergarten; now I could be the mom who took her kids to school and the mom who had a career.

As scary as it was to take that leap, it was truly the best thing I have ever done career-wise. I left my job with just a few hours of project work lined up with a colleague's air quality consulting firm. And I never looked back.

Lesson 5:
Women Have to Fight for Leadership Roles—and I'm Not a Fighter

I learned a valuable lesson during those eighteen years in corporate America: there was little room for women in advanced positions, and I had neither the ability nor the interest in fighting for one of the few leadership spots available to someone like me.

So instead I carved out my own niche and did what made me happy. There have been ups and downs and I have learned and changed so much. Seventeen years have elapsed since I took the leap to go out on my own. Instead of fighting for a leadership role in corporate America, I have learned that there are other ways to lead—like building a company and writing a book.

CREATING A SUSTAINABLE SELF CAN HELP US CREATE A SUSTAINABLE WORLD

The same philosophies we use to improve ourselves are the same ones we can use to improve our environment. What creates a sustainable self creates a sustainable world.

Over the course of ten weeks, we can make a real difference in achieving the balance in our lives that allows us to do better and be better.

There are 7.7 billion people in the world and more than one billion of them live in developed countries.[1] Imagine what would happen if the people enjoying the good life decided to be more mindful of how our everyday choices affect the rest of the world and what we are leaving for the next generation.

We are living in a society that uses items, which are designed to last hundreds of years, just one time and then throws them away. From the 150 million tons of plastic produced every year, more than eight million tons end up in our oceans. One in three species of marine mammals have been found entangled in our discarded materials and over 90 percent of all seabirds have some plastic in their guts.[2] And even worse than the ocean gyres of plastics, teeny-tiny, nanosized bits are making their way into the food chain—and thus us.[3]

Surely we can do better.

And we want to do better.

And then there's work, kids, finances, commuting, health

issues, caregiving for family members—the list goes on and on.

But we are hopeful, so we wake up each day and carry on.

This book puts intention behind that hopefulness. In ten weeks, I believe you can be a better you and thus help create a better planet. Why ten weeks? Because science tells us it takes a little more than two months, give or take, to adopt a new behavior.[4]

Don't worry, we'll start small. Like how to remove single-use plastics from everyday use. In learning how to tackle little things, we will learn the skills to tackle much bigger issues as well, like the really big one of our time: climate change.

IF I CAN DO IT, SO CAN YOU

Using anecdotes from my personal journey through breast cancer, and drawing on my science background and general curiosity about everything, I have meshed together the science that will help us get our lives back in balance so that we can do things that matter for the environment. Better people, better planet.

How to Use This Book

As I worked my way back from the deconditioning (decreased physical capacity) that resulted from chemotherapy, I gained a clear understanding of the foundational elements we need in our lives to get the balance that living to our potential requires.

These elements became the basis for the chapters in this book.

Each of the ten chapters is equivalent to one week and focuses on some aspect of how we can be better and do better. They are intended to be connected and each one builds on the previous chapters. Every week's concept is based on science and real-world experience.

This information is connected in a way that can be applied to our lives, our families, our homes, and our communities. There is no silver bullet or one size fits all. In every case you have to figure out what works for you. Hopefully in leading by example, you'll get some ideas from my story.

This process starts with small steps. These small steps are the beginning of a journey that could very well take you to a place you had never imagined, doing more than you might have ever believed possible.

The order of these chapters is intentional so be sure to follow them sequentially. Ideally, you will only read one chapter each week, put the concepts into practice for seven days or so, and then move on to the next chapter the following week. During subsequent weeks, you will keep practicing the concepts from the prior weeks. This allows you to build and grow a foundation of better practices that enable a better life and that are also sustainable for the rest of your life. As you progress, your eyes will be opened to possibilities you walked right past before.

I imagine each week of practice as a stream of water. As the subsequent weeks are added, the flow grows stronger until after ten weeks, you have the power of a river propelling you along.

If you are having trouble with the practices from one week, repeat them. Likewise, if you have already integrated one of the concepts, review it for a refresher and move on. After all, the concept that it takes ten weeks to make a habit automatic is really an average. It could be several days less or several days more to make any one of these a part of the rhythm of your life.

And if the way this is presented doesn't resonate with you, no worries; try another way, your way, and keep trying until you find what works for you.

Success does not require perfection. One little misstep does not mean failure.[5] Every day is an opportunity to try again.

How the Book Is Organized

Each of the chapters are linked:

- Week 1: Sleep . . . so you can play.
- Week 2: Play . . . so you can be.
- Week 3: Be . . . so you can spend.
- Week 4: Spend . . . so you can serve.
- Week 5: Serve . . . so you can shed.
- Week 6: Shed . . . so you can stretch.
- Week 7: Stretch . . . so you can inhabit.
- Week 8: Inhabit . . . so you can make space.

- Week 9: Make space . . . so you can share.
- Week 10: Share . . . to make better people and a better planet.

After all that, there is a bonus section on science. With so much seemingly conflicting information out there, it can be hard to make sense in the chaos. Borrowing from experts in the field, I give you a recipe for exactly how to do just that.

There are actions you can take for yourself and the environment at the end of each chapter, identified as "Find Your Rhythm." And if those small sustainability challenges at the end of each chapter are not enough, check out the list of "Shifts and Swaps" at the end of the book.

This planet called Earth doesn't need us, but we sure need this planet. When we find ourselves at the "last straw," the one that broke the camel's back, the next steps in the journey of our lives become crystal clear. With that clarity, we can find the conviction to do what needs to be done to take care of ourselves and the environment.

SHARE YOUR JOURNEY

As you embark on this journey, I want to hear from you. Share your successes and seek support for your struggles from a like-minded community. Find the Facebook page titled "The Last Straw Book" and join the group "The Last Straw." Also check our website, thelaststrawbook.com, from time to time for more information.

So, let's get past the last straw—in your life, and the one we use for drinks, too.

WEEK 1: SLEEP

"I've always envied people who sleep easily. Their brains must be cleaner, the floorboards of the skull well swept, all the little monsters closed up in a steamer trunk at the foot of the bed."

– David Benioff, *The City of Thieves*

My family tells me that I was a very good sleeper as a child—so good that as a toddler playing with my little cousins, my mom would say, "Where's Joycie?" She'd then come to find me underfoot of the others, toys strewn all over the floor, lying fast asleep in the midst of it. I do love sleep.

But you're probably saying, seriously, your big entrance to this book is sleep? Yep. Getting enough sleep makes everything else possible, and if you have not gotten enough sleep in the past, it can be life changing.

In this chapter, I'll share my sleep story—going from a brilliant sleeper to brilliantly sleep deprived—and hopefully there will be some aspect that resonates with you and helps you improve your ability to sleep well. Once we have the foundation of sleep, we can begin to find balance in other parts of our daily life.

WE DON'T MISS SLEEP UNTIL WE CAN'T GET IT

In 2017, at a routine mammogram, a mass was discovered in my right breast. So, I did what needed to be done and got on with life. Except, after the surgery, and the chemo, and the radiation, and more than a year of recovery, I went from being a brilliant sleeper to just plain tired. I was tired all the time. So tired. I stayed in bed up to ten hours a night reaching for that elusive feeling that only comes with a good night's rest. I took afternoon naps. I went to bed early. I slept late. I frequently woke up with headaches. I felt like I was in a fog.

There were slight (sometimes not so slight) pauses in conversation as I searched to recall the word I was looking for. I was asked to pass the salt and handed over a butter knife. I made plans for New Year's Eve and forgot them. I attended a motivational speaker event and even though it was still going strong and I was very engaged, my body said no more at 5 p.m. and I had to walk out. Visiting a friend in Colorado, I got to bed at 4 a.m. after delays from a snowstorm; getting just four hours of sleep that night, it took ten days before I felt quasi-normal again (that is, just tired, instead of walking-dead tired).

I was fifty-six years old and wondered, so is that it? Am I done? Am I old? Am I just waiting it out now?

Fatigue, chemo brain, deconditioning—all of these are very real and lasting effects of chemotherapy. Only in conducting research for this book did I learn that "twelve weeks of chemotherapy is equivalent to a decade of cardiorespiratory fitness decline."[6] No wonder I was still tired!

I needed help, but I wasn't so much afraid of asking as I was of the answer.

DON'T BE AFRAID TO GET PROFESSIONAL HELP

So, on a routine follow-up visit to my oncologist, I asked, "Can this *still* be the effect of the chemo?" She asked a few questions, considered my age, and responded, "You need a sleep study."

I knew I had some kind of apnea because I was aware enough during sleep to know that at times I was waking myself when my airway closed. I was limited to two sleeping in two very price positions on either side: the pillow tucked between my neck and shoulder, bottom arm parallel to the pillow, elbow bent, fist anchored in the opposite shoulder, wrist under chin, bottom jaw pressed forward—all trying to keep my airway open while I slept. I knew there was a problem, but I did not want one of those ugly, noisy, ill-fitting, decidedly un-sexy CPAP machines.[7]

I did the sleep study—at home—and it was not nearly as

disruptive as I thought it might be. The kit included a finger probe to measure oxygen saturation, a cannula under my nose to measure airflow, and sensors on my chest to measure chest rise and fall and heart rate—all stored in a data device.

They were able to get enough data to make a diagnosis of mild obstructive sleep apnea, based on the average number of events per hour when I stopped breathing for ten seconds or more.[8] And of course, not breathing is bad because when we aren't breathing, our body is not getting oxygen. I was surprised to find it is normal to have up to five of these events an hour. In other words, it is normal to stop breathing several times an hour when sleeping! Thirty or more events is categorized as severe.[9] Imagine not breathing thirty times in an hour, ten seconds each time. You would be missing out on five minutes of sleep each hour! I didn't even have the most severe sleep apnea and it was dramatically affecting my life.

So I ended up with an APAP machine (an automatic, as opposed to a continuous, positive airway pressure device) and it was *instantly* life changing.[10] In an interview about her movie *Wine Country*, former *Saturday Night Live* cast member Amy Poehler said this about bringing her CPAP machine onto the movie set: "It has completely changed my life . . . I've always been a terrible sleeper. I performed most of my career incredibly sleep deprived . . . It's the best thing I've ever done for my health. So yeah, much like my friend Bradley Cooper, who used his real dog in *A Star Is Born*, I used my real CPAP machine in this movie."[11]

Thank you, Amy! If a famous actress/writer/producer like Amy Poehler can own it, so can I.

Luckily, I didn't need the big honking mouth and nose covering mask Amy used in *Wine Country* (sorry Amy!), just a quiet, lightweight piece that puts air through my nose. I call it my sleep machine, and it is streamlined, nice looking, and my very best friend. I do not feel any air pressure at all when it is on, but it blows like a windstorm when I take it off. If I open my mouth, there's a little bit of Darth Vader going on as air rushes out.

Yes, occasionally I feel like I am wrestling an octopus when the unnecessarily long, looping length of tubing doesn't move with me, and I have been known to get entangled in my phone cord, Kindle charger cord, *and* APAP hose in hotels— but I always find my way out, and it's worth it because this one amazing device gave me my life back. I wake up after almost exactly eight hours and I am rested. No more morning headaches! I have the energy to work out! I make plans and keep them! I don't search for words! I have IDEAS again! I AM BACK!

My sleep machine even helped with my dreams. I often remember my dreams upon waking; that had stopped entirely during sleep-deprived time. Dreaming is important in helping ideas coalesce and clarify. Joy Harjo, our US poet laureate says,

"It's important to have a doorway open to the place without words, and that happens more easily when you've come from dreaming."[12] The science supports this. A review of studies on dreams and sleep apnea published in *Frontiers in Neurology* suggests that sleep apnea can affect dream recall and dream content.[13] My conclusion: To dream big, sleep well!

To dream big, sleep well.

START WITH A SLEEP BUDGET

Anyone who has spent interrupted nights with a newborn knows just how important sleep is. I remember those first weeks back at work after having my babies, just wishing the day would end so that I could start fresh and try again tomorrow, hopefully with more energy after better rest. Sorting for recycling, reusable water bottles, and alternatives to disposable diapers were the last things on my mind—if they crossed my mind at all.

We know we need more sleep, but we often underestimate the impact insufficient sleep can have on us. Twenty percent of all American adults show some signs of chronic sleep deprivation. Not getting enough sleep can contribute to weight gain, cardio-vascular issues, and memory issues.[14] I can vouch for all three.

If you have bragging rights for how little sleep you can get by on, or if you have ever said, "I'll sleep when I'm dead!" you're getting it wrong. We need good sleep each night in order to have the energy to be our best each day.[15] Sleep helps our creativity, our problem-solving, our memory, and our performance,[16] but if you need to be persuaded that sleep is the most important part of your day (or night), try listening to Dr. Matthew Carter's TEDx Talk, "The Science of Sleep (and the Art of Productivity)."[17]

Just like a financial budget can help us get to our money-related goals faster, a sleep budget can help get us to our life goals faster. There are twenty-four hours in a day and eight of them (give or take a few for your body's requirements) should be spent sleeping. Start with budgeting enough sleep, and then fit everything else in around that.

Make sleep a priority.

FIGURE OUT WHAT WORKS FOR YOU

If you need help with getting to sleep or staying asleep, there is plenty of advice available about reducing caffeine intake late in the day, avoiding alcohol, exercising, and limiting screen time just before bedtime.

For me, after I cozy up in bed, a mental rundown of the day followed by a silent acknowledgment on the thing I am most grateful for works every time. For waking at night, the advice is to do something rather than attempting to force yourself to sleep.

For me, reading on my Kindle works well—so well sometimes it conks me on the forehead as I fall asleep with it resting on my chest. For others, meditation or prayer is effective.

If you're having problems, here are some more specific tips:

1. Increase bright light exposure during the day.
2. Reduce blue light exposure (from smartphones, tablets, and computers) in the evening.
3. Reserve caffeine for early in the day (six to eight hours before bedtime).
4. Reduce daytime naps (except power naps of thirty minutes or less).
5. Try to sleep and wake at consistent times.
6. Don't drink alcohol.
7. Optimize your bedroom for temperature, noise, and lights.
8. Don't eat or drink too late.
9. Create a relaxing nighttime routine that works for you (music, reading, bath or shower, meditation, gratitude recitation).
10. Do some physical activity, but not right before bed.
11. If you are already physically activity, then up the level and be sure and break a sweat.
12. Get the right mattress, pillows, and bed linens.[18]

And if you have seemingly insurmountable sleep issues, then maybe a sleep study is in your future, too. It's really not so bad, especially since you can do it at home in your own bed.

FIND YOUR RHYTHM

In the introduction, I promised actions you can take for yourself and the environment at the end of each chapter. Once you get sleep down cold, maybe you can use your newfound energy to start making some small changes that move you toward more sustainable environmental habits.

> For You

Work on getting better at sleeping well this week. Keep a sleep journal every night this week; write down when you go to bed, when you wake up, how much activity (physical and screen time), how much food and caffeine you have in the six hours preceding bedtime, and any other information (for example, stressors) that relate to the amount of sleep you are (or aren't) getting.

Based on this information, adjust your sleep habits using the list from this chapter. If you can't resolve your sleep issues over the course of a few weeks, make an appointment with your physician to figure out why that is. In the meantime, keep making changes in your lifestyle to see if they help.

> For the Environment

Swap this for that. Choose at least one single-use, plastic item and eliminate it from your life. Our parents or grandparents managed just fine without these items.

- Swap plastic grocery bags for reusable cloth bags or paper bags in a pinch
- Swap single-use, plastic water bottles for reusable water bottles
- Swap Styrofoam coffee cups for reusable mugs
- And of course, swap plastic straws for no straws, paper straws, bamboo or stainless steel straws, or other reusable straws

Too easy? Already following these practices? Check out the "Shifts and Swaps" at the end of the book for more ideas.

Sleep makes everything better. Sleep makes everything possible. Getting enough sleep allows us to have the energy and the desire to change our habits for the better. If you want to be a better citizen of the world, if you want more sustainable practices in your life, start by getting enough sleep.

So, if incorporating an alternative to plastic straws in your life, or separating out recyclables from trash seems insurmount-able, there's a very good chance you need more sleep.

Sleep . . . so you can play! Because when you get enough rest, anything is possible. With enough sleep, you might even feel like making time to play.

WEEK 2: PLAY

"The opposite of work is not play, it is depression."

– Brian Sutton-Smith

I am not very good at playing. I was as good as the next kid as a child: trying to make booby-trapped haunted houses in the barn, playing kickball during recess, riding my bike, playing catch, catching fireflies in the twilight, swimming the summer away, and traipsing about in the woods.

What happened? I don't try to make haunted houses, play kickball, ride my bike, play catch, catch fireflies, or even swim very much anymore.

Does it really matter? I'm an adult with adult responsibilities and I really don't have time for play, right?

When we play, we find joy. (Just describing my childhood play made me feel it!) We relax. We become more open to doing the work that is required to create and maintain sustainable habits, like using a reusable water bottle instead of a single-use, plastic bottle.

Now that we are (hopefully) on the way to sleeping well, the day is looking much brighter. We have more energy and can make time to play, building balance back into our lives one step at a time.

In this chapter, we'll explain why play is so important for adults, and how to remind ourselves what play looks like for us. I didn't realize it at the time, but play had an important role in creating some of the normalcy I craved during my chemo days.

PLAY MATTERS

According to Dr. Stuart Brown, the authority on play, "adults who embrace fully their inherent play nature" have a better quality of life, decreased stress, are better connected to their communities, and are more likely to foster empathy and maintain their optimism in a changing, challenging, and demanding world.[19] Sounds a lot like the world we're living in right now, doesn't it?

What even is "play" when you are an adult? Dr. Brown defines play as "purposeless, fun, and pleasurable." There is no goal. It is not necessary for one's daily existence. It is enjoyable and in the moment.[20]

It took a bit of thinking to spot play in my adult life. I realized that the puttering about my husband and I do on the weekends is a form of play. We spend time outdoors doing this or that as we feel like it, with no real motivation other than to be outside. Sometimes I just follow a butterfly or dragonfly as far as I can, or I pause, mesmerized by a caterpillar in the early stages of forming a chrysalis or by the sandhill cranes, egrets, or ducks that come into our yard.

Another example of play for my husband is bicycling. But for me, bicycling is torture—at least the way he does it (many miles, many hours in the saddle). So play will be different for each of us.

We might have to reconnect with our child self to re-connect with play.

FINDING MY WAY BACK TO PLAY

What I recall most as a child is wandering about aimlessly in the woods across from our home. The houses were spaced far apart, and there were few other kids to play with. Ten safe acres of woods across the dusty gravel road became my playground. There were box turtles, mayapples, and jacks-in-the-pulpit in spring. If you were really lucky, you might find those beautiful, tiny, tree-like morel mushrooms my mom would prepare by soaking them in salt water (to remove the bugs that might have been inside), slicing them in half, dipping them in flour, and then pan-frying them. Oh, how I miss those!

After all this time, nothing restores me like being outdoors. I guess I do still have play in my life, it just looks a little different.

Now, play is when my sixty-eight-year-old friend Polly and I traipse through the woods like ten-year-old girls. This time exploring nature with my friend was key to making me feel like a normal person during and after chemo. Two days after my first chemo, we went on a birding hike with her amateur ornithologist friends. I learned to distinguish the crested caracara (or Mexican eagle) from the black vulture during this hike.

Later in the summer, it was hot and humid and by then I was very bald. I would swap my wig for a ball cap and we'd head out into the woods; there was no one to notice my hairless state, and I was careful to apply plenty of sunscreen. I had to sleep for a couple of hours afterwards, but it was worth it to get that little bit of normalcy—play, as it turns out—in my life.

The last time we explored some of her property, ever in search of the ancient alligator turtle she had spotted another time, we followed a snowy egret as it searched the shallow edges of the cattail-laden slough. We watched a great blue heron we stumbled upon taking flight and saw three deer pause, stock-still, to see what we would do next before taking off from the open meadow into the safety of the woods.

So now I know that play is when my husband and I hike through our fifty, very rough acres of wild hog and huisache-infested property to the sandy beach on the Brazos River, which sits across from three stories of red, orange, and brown-layered sediment cut by the mighty river during flood stage.

Play is when we take a walk through the Åmosen nature preserve and wetlands near my husband's childhood home in Denmark. The preserve is sprinkled with quaint, thatch-roofed homes that surely the Danish equivalent of Hansel and Gretel must have visited, and tall pine forests so dense they are dark inside even during the day, smelling like Christmas. Our feet sound so quiet on the layers of pine needles and moss, it's like being in a fairy-tale land holding tiny baby pine trees in a forest nursery. When we are lucky, we hear a pheasant or see a fox, hare, deer, or hedgehog.

When I can't make it to the woods, I listen to podcasts while walking in my neighborhood and picking up trash or puttering around in my yard. I keep an eye out to enjoy the green anoles, skinks, snakes, tree frogs, toads, cardinals, blue jays, hawks, armadillos, raccoons, opossums, skunks, red-eared slider turtles, egrets, herons, sandhill cranes, and black-bellied whistling tree ducks that make their way in, around, and above our home.

Being in nature is my play.

When we really see nature, we learn to love it, and we want to protect what we love.

YOU NEVER KNOW WHERE PLAY MIGHT TAKE YOU

I mentioned that during my walks, quite often I pick up litter. Yes, even picking up trash is rejuvenating for me. Well, not so much the picking up part as the results of seeing a litter-free environment. I enjoy sorting the recyclables from the trash and making sure the aluminum cans find their way back into the production stream. In the US, we throw away more than $700 million worth of aluminum cans every year, when aluminum is 100 percent recyclable![21]

I've very much internalized the habit of picking up trash, despite my family's eye-rolling and protests during family walks ("Please don't stop and pick up trash *this* time!"). But even I have my limits. When my daughter, Kaitlin, was four, she went to pick up a particularly disgusting piece of tire-flattened food waste in a parking lot. I quickly explained that there were store workers who would collect it, and it was okay for us to leave it there. Sometimes it's the safest option to leave the litter where it is, even though we really want to help it find its proper home.

My problem is that I don't just see the plastic water bottle or aluminum can on the ground; I imagine the whole chain of how it got here and where it's going to end up and what a waste of natural resources it is.

I imagine the energy required to make it, from the coal mining that leveled a mountaintop and disrupted an entire ecosystem, to the coal's transport by rail to the power plant, where it is burned and scrubbed, but still leaves mercury and other pollutants in the air and deposited in the soil, on crops, and in our lungs.

I imagine that plastic grocery bag making its way to the creek behind our house during one of the frog-stranglers all too common in Texas, then to the Brazos River, and finally to the Gulf of Mexico where a dolphin or turtle thinks it's a jellyfish for eating.

I imagine the nicotine from cigarette butts casually tossed out a car window potentially poisoning the gophers, mice, and shrews on which birds of prey survive. Or a momma bird feeding its baby plastic bits, thinking they are food, or a turtle becoming entangled in balloon string.

I just can't let that happen, not on my watch. I love keeping our neighborhood neat and clean for all the beautiful children riding bikes and scooters or walking, skipping, and running between the houses as they visit their little friends to play.

They deserve it and so do you.

There will always be some of us who start out playing and end up working. That's okay. As long as we are finding joy in what we do, even if it's preventing litter from impacting our environment, we've got the right idea.

FIGURE OUT WHAT WORKS FOR YOU

If you are having trouble figuring out what kind of play is for you, Dr. Brown suggests that you make a play history for yourself. Go back to your earliest memory of play. Take that memory and find what you do now that aligns with that.

Or watch your kids at play and take ideas from them—or even join them. One of my fondest memories of my dad is when us kids were trying, and failing, to walk on our hands out in the yard. He had finished chores on our little farm and was wearing heavy leather boots caked with hog manure. Without saying a word, he dropped the bucket he was carrying, went into a handstand, and began walking on his hands, muddy boots in the air. My dad worked a lot—all day and every evening—but at that moment he joined us in play, and I remember it fifty years later. My dad is gone, but that moment of pure joyful play will stay with me forever.

Need more inspiration on play? Check out Dr. Brown's TED talk, "Play is More than Just Fun."[22]

Bonus: Some kinds of play will help get you in the 150 minutes per week of moderate-intensity aerobic activity that the American Heart Association recommends.[23] And physical activity is bound to help you sleep better; it definitely works for me.

Make time to play.

FIND YOUR RHYTHM

Work on making time for play in your life this week, and then see if you can swap out another small thing in your life for something more sustainable.

> For You

Experiment with play this week, whatever that might look like: LEGOs with the kids, knitting, ping pong, hiking, biking, running, playing tennis, frisbee, tag, tumbling, board games, charades, play wrestling, tickling your kids, or whatever sounds fun to you. What did you find? Can you incorporate that into a regular part of your daily or weekly rhythm?

> For the Environment

Swap this for that. Building on last week's success, choose one more single-use, plastic item and eliminate it from your life. Here are some ideas:

- Swap plastic produce bags for nothing or reusable produce or cloth bags
- Swap plastic or Styrofoam packaging with cardboard or paper packaging for eggs or aluminum for soft drinks and other products that you buy (that is, base your purchase on the packaging)

- Swap plastic wrap for reusable glass jars with metal lids or glass containers with reusable plastic lids

So if the idea of taking your own reusable bags to the store annoys you, or unplugging your charger cords when not in use seems too small an effort to bother with, maybe you need to go out and . . . play. Who can be cranky after a good bit of joyful play?

Play . . . so you can be! If you build play into your life, you will be on a path to finding your best you.

WEEK 3: BE

"Be yourself; everyone else is already taken."

– Oscar Wilde

The election of Barack Obama was heralded as a historic moment because he was an African-American. I contend that the truly historic moment will be when no one comments on the ethnicity, skin color, gender, sexual orientation, or religion of our president or any elected official because that will mean it's not an issue.

We have a long way to go.

Likewise, diversity and inclusion in the workplace is typically illustrated by a United Colors of Benetton rainbow of people, as if having a light-skinned person and a dark-skinned person, a heterosexual and a homosexual, a woman and a man, a Muslim and a Christian, and any other combination you can think of will inherently bring the differences we need to make for a stronger team or business. It does seem intuitive that it would. And given the historical lack of opportunities for "others," it is long overdue and worth every bit of effort, persistence, and tenacity it takes.

However, we will only have true diversity and inclusion when these types of categories and differences are accepted without thinking, and we are looking more deeply to differences in ways of being.

CULTURAL DIVERSITY IS NOT ENOUGH

We hear a lot of talk about authenticity in the workplace: "Be your authentic self." But do we even know what our authentic self is? After so many years of trying to conform to expectations—or trying to rebel against them—and all of the pressures we feel coming at us from social media, religion, politics, family, community, and elsewhere, I'm not sure we can know what our authentic self is.

Being our authentic self is also the key to unlocking the door to our preferred way of doing better by the environment. When we align our actions to our natural way of being, we are more likely to succeed, no matter the goal.

I have come across a couple of things that helped me a lot and I believe they can help you, too. The first is related to rediscovering your natural way of being and the second is understanding how you manage conflict.

Rediscovering your natural way of being will get you to a

place where your actions are more aligned with what works best for you (and it just feels right). Understanding how you manage conflict will help you to work with and influence others, without sacrificing your needs.

Discovering my natural way of being allowed me to write this book. It would have never happened otherwise. Understanding how to manage conflict has brought me to a place where I am better able to positively influence others—no one is scolded, shamed, or embarrassed into sustainable habits.

Let's find your natural way of being, and give you some tools to manage conflict, too.

FINDING YOUR NATURAL WAY TO *BE*

As it turns out, there were a few more stories that I had knitted into my life that needed unraveling before I could get back to my natural way of being.

Stories from My School Years

I was a typical child except in the ways I wasn't. I liked school. I liked it so much that in third grade, I asked for—and received—workbooks for Christmas. What kid wants more schoolwork *for Christmas*?! In fourth grade, the class worked hard to cover a huge roll of butcher paper with a colorful drawing of a cross-section of a coal mine. I enjoyed this activity so much that I created a report on coal mining on loose-leaf paper complete with red yarn tied in little bows to hold the papers together. There was no assignment, no extra credit—I created my own extra credit. They say memories are tied to strong emotions, and I remember feeling so proud when my teacher, Mrs. O'Neal, showed it to my mom. Aha! We get rewarded for doing extra, even if it was just play to us.

When extra credit artwork was given in our science class in eighth grade—the assignment was a pencil drawing of a pinecone and gingko leaf, to be judged by the art teacher—I won. My science teacher was ticked. This project was intended to give other, struggling students a way to improve their grades, which I did not need. I felt bad about doing well. I should have skipped that bit of extra credit to let others have a chance. I figured, this is me, doing the work, and missing the social cues. Aha! Sometimes doing extra, even just for fun, gets punished.

Even though I attended a small high school, we were fortunate to have some exceptional educators. There were two I remember vividly; one because of his support of my nerdy self and my interest in science, and our junior year English teacher who had a reputation for being no nonsense, despite her diminutive stature. Talk about scared straight, there was no disruption in that classroom. I sat near the front of the class to the right, and one morning as she was giving a lecture on grammar, I decided to organize my notebook, very quietly. After all, I knew I could both listen and organize. At one point, our teacher stopped, made a comment about people being rude, and I had sense enough to look up but noticed she was staring straight ahead. Since she wasn't looking at me, I breathed a sigh of relief and carried on. Except, of course, she *was* directing her comment at me. Aha! Sometimes being efficient is not only not rewarded, it can be considered rude.

We spend a lot of time, especially in adolescence, thinking something is wrong with us. For all these years, I have thought of myself not as just an introverted nerd, but also as someone who is not very perceptive. That's my authentic self. Not much to work with but I've somehow made a go of it.

Understanding Our Natural Way of Being

And then it was like a window into me was opened and I could see that I was so much more than just an introverted nerd. At the suggestion of a colleague who went on her own personal journey of discovery, I took the Kolbe A Index.[24] I'm always up for a personality test, so it was an easy sell; however, this was different. Instead of an IQ test (thinking) or a personality type (feeling), the Kolbe test is used to define our preferred method of being (doing). If we shed all of the constraints on how we think we need to *perform* or *be*, that is, if we align our behaviors with our natural state, then we will *perform* at our best and *be* our happiest.

Kolbe defines and ranks four action modes:

- Fact Finder
- Follow Thru
- Quick Start
- Implementor

The more the way you are allowed to work aligns with your preferred action mode, the happier you will be and the better you will perform; the less aligned, the more stressful it will be to perform well.

After you take the Kolbe A Index, the first thing you will be told is, "You have a perfect score!" In other words, there is no profile that is right or wrong, better or worse, stronger or weaker. So if you are not a fan of these types of tests, fear not! There will be nothing for you to feel bad about.

I was really surprised to find out that my preferred mode is Quick Start. Being an introverted, technical nerd, I thought I would have scored high on Fact Finder and Follow Thru. In fact, I was performing in this way to such a great extent that others in my life who have done the Kolbe A Index tell me that they thought I was a Fact Finder and Follow Thru, too!

Turns out that those were roles I was performing because the need to make a living and support my family required it. The profile explained why I am easily bored with the *status quo* and always searching for the next interesting thing. It was why I was asking for workbooks for Christmas when I was eight; why I was doing independent research when I was nine; why I took on the challenge of drawing for extra credit I didn't need when I was twelve; why I was working hard to stay engaged in a class lecture by doing another task at the same time when I was fifteen. It is why my small business has managed to stay afloat for more than seventeen years, as I constantly reinvent myself by obtaining additional training to help my clients, finding new ways to reach new customers, and working in a variety of collaborations and partnerships.

I was a Quick Start who had been born into a slow life! No wonder I never really fit in.

Permission to *Be*

Understanding my preferred mode of operation granted me permission to value the part of myself that likes to move quickly, generate ideas, try and fail and try again, and learn what works and what doesn't—and for that to be okay. Letting go of my fear of failure (or judgment) was a big one. So now rather than stuffing down those big ideas I have, many more than I can possibly do, I am grateful for them. When ideas keep me from sleeping or pop into my head when I wake up, I jot them down on a pad of paper I keep on my nightstand; for the ones that come to me in the car or at my desk, I capture them on my phone or in my idea book. Maybe one of these ideas will become something one day. Maybe not. But I am owning them instead of disregarding them as not worthy or not relevant or not practical or too difficult. Maybe one day, when the time is right, I will come back to them.

Just as important, I was able to let go of feeling bad about myself because I am not very good at making or repairing or building things. Cooking, making crafts, even decorating for the holidays—these are all like pulling teeth for me. Thankfully for our family, my husband is an excellent cook and very handy (my guess, an Implementor).

Finding the Path to *Being*

With 13 percent of employed Americans reporting they are actively disengaged at work and three in ten saying their job is "just a job to get them by," doing what we can to align our natural state of being with our work can only lead to something better for everyone.[25] I wonder what would have happened if I had discovered and accepted my true state sooner in my career. So much of what led to my success was brute force—putting in the hours, getting the work done, even when the work was absolutely mind numbing. That's what got me to this point of making a good living, sending my kids to college, having a second home and property.

But when I aligned myself to even just a little bit of my

true nature—like I did when I took the big leap from corporate America to independent consulting—I put in less time, had less stress, and made more money.

Even though I enjoyed and grew from every position I had, it was still a grind. Working through the week for the reward of social events on Friday night, laundry and chores over the weekend, more fun on Saturday night, then the dread of Sunday night, knowing Monday was just around the corner was. And by the way, the laundry still wasn't done. It was exhausting!

Now I avoid the traffic, work when it makes sense based on my energy level (for the most part), get enough sleep, incorporate some play and volunteering, and am so much happier.

But the independent consulting has had its share of working for the money as opposed to the enjoyment. As the kids have left the nest, with more time available, I have been struggling to find joy in the escapes, like puttering outside, that used to restore me after a workweek.

Now that I am making space for other things, like writing, I feel fulfilled in a way I haven't before. I believe this is what it looks like for me to be in my natural state of Quick Start. I have stopped apologizing (to myself) for being an idea person and I work harder to communicate clearly to others who might misunderstand my ideas as directives, that these are only ideas—not suggestions or judgments. Sometimes, it feels like I need a yellow triangle that says, "Caution: Watch out for Falling Ideas!"

How to *Be* for the Environment

If you want to integrate better environmental practices into your life, take advantage of your preferred way of being and doing, and you will have an easier path:

- Fact Finder: If you like to get as many specifics as possible, research the best environmental options. Review life-cycle assessments. Share your research with the rest of us so we can benefit from the results of what comes naturally to you and then we can also do better.
- Follow Thru: If you like to design systems that organize everything, then find ways to make being a good environmental steward easier. Create systems in your home, work, and community that make doing good easy.
- Quick Start: If you are an idea person who likes to test and experiment (you are comfortable with uncertainty), then test your environmental ideas and don't be afraid to fail and try again.
- Implementor: If you like to make things, then your skills are definitely needed in creating practical engineering and technology solutions for environmental problems.

How to *Be* with Others

It's definitely great to understand and work within your preferred action mode, but others in your life may work differently. There can be challenges and even conflicts in your home, work, or community when you offer up new ways of doing things. For this, we need to understand our conflict management style and that of others as well.

UNDERSTANDING YOUR WAY OF MANAGING CONFLICT

I really hate conflict. So much so that I will do almost anything to avoid it. It's been a real struggle for me to figure out how to deal with the outspoken, in-your-face type of person that bull-dozes through life, creating a wake of collateral damage that leaves the rest of us feeling dismissed or disrespected. And then I discovered the science behind conflict management.

Know Your Conflict Management Style

As with so many things in my life, the way of understanding how I deal with conflict fell into my lap—was actually assigned to me—while completing my master's degree some twenty years after I started it. I took a course on leadership that introduced me to the "Thomas-Kilmann Conflict Mode Instrument"[26] (TKI) and the companion booklet, *Introduction to Conflict and Teams.*[27]

Thomas and the Kilmanns introduce us to five team member conflict styles based on the level of cooperativeness (thinking of others) versus assertiveness (thinking of one's self):

- Uncooperative and unassertive = Avoider
- Cooperative and unassertive = Accommodator
- Uncooperative and assertive = Competitor
- Cooperative and assertive = Collaborator
- In the middle = Compromiser

I completed the TKI and ranked 88th percentile in the mode of avoiding and 74th percentile in the mode of collaborating. Compromising and accommodating were my third and fourth preferred modes, and my least preferred mode was competing at the 20th percentile. No surprise on the avoidance, but revelatory on the collaboration. Collaboration brings a natural state of high for me and is my preferred method of conflict resolution (because there is no conflict!). It seems that when I cannot collaborate, I avoid. Having this information helped me understand that there are times when it is appropriate for me to avoid less and compete more, and the information provided with the profile showed me how to manage other styles based on my own preferred modes.

For people like me who really don't like conflict, this self-knowledge can help us step up in authentic ways when needed. For those who go straight to compromise every time (there was one classmate like this), the profile shows there are other, potentially better, options to try first. Likewise, if you are always accommodating, there is a good chance that your needs are not being met much of the time. And finally, for those who compete every time a conflict arises and wonder why they are winning the battles but losing the war, this self-evaluation can be critical to their future success. Self-knowledge is essential for conflict management, and a plan for handling difficult conversations will help you put that into place.

Planning for Difficult Conversations

In his book *Conversational Capacity,* Craig Weber gives us a four-part plan for those challenging moments when we find ourselves in the middle of a difficult conversation:

- *State* our position clearly, concisely, and succinctly.
- *Explain* the underlying thinking that informs the position, with data and how we have interpreted that data.
- *Test* our perspective by asking for feedback.
- *Inquire* into the perspectives of others.[28]

Weber thinks of it this way, "The first two skills bring structure to our candor; the second two balance it with curiosity. Combined, they produce a user-friendly framework for crafting conversations that are simultaneously candid and curious." It sounds so simple, and it is if you can avoid the traps of minimizing and devaluing your own views, trying to win, and responding to feedback and others' perspectives with negativity instead of curiosity. Years ago, I heard someone in customer service say, "don't get mad, get curious," which aligns nicely with Weber's model. When applied, it can remind us to listen more than we speak.

For example, you might use this process in a discussion with your resistant partner on whether to get solar panels.

- State your position: *I'm looking into solar panels for our home.*
- Explain your underlying thinking: *There's a federal tax credit and maybe we can even sell power back to the grid. We'll be paying about the same as our current electric bill, and there's no down payment required.*
- Ask for feedback: *What are your thoughts? Am I missing anything?*
- Inquire with others: *Let's check in with our neighbor and see what their experience was like when they got solar panels.*

If you're a Quick Start paired with a Fact Finder, you're in luck! If intrigued, your Fact Finder partner will do all of the research.

There is also the "I feel ____ when ____. I'd really like it if _____" statement developed by Thomas Gordon.[29] For example, "I feel really bummed about how much food goes into the trash every week. I'd really like it if we could brainstorm ways to reduce our food waste. What do you think?" (Instead of, "You always throw away so much food! It's such a waste.")

"I" statements allow us to articulate and take responsibility for our feelings, communicate them, and then suggest changes that aren't delivered in a way that makes the recipient defensive. A *caveat*: while this is great in certain situations, in my experience it is not well received at work (depending on office culture), and definitely not good to use with an individual with a dominant competitor conflict management profile. With them, it is like exposing your soft underbelly!

Sometimes I wonder how it would have gone down with my competitor boss seventeen years ago when I ended up leaving what started as my dream job. Something tells me we could have both benefited from this kind of self-awareness. Conflict management is something I know I will work on for the rest of my life. I will always be seeking the natural state of high that comes with collaboration—those moments when your team has tossed out so many ideas and built on them, that by the end, you have no idea where credit resides because it was truly a team effort. I just need to avoid interacting less with those whose preferred mode is competing. These are mostly family members, not work colleagues!

Align your life to your natural way of
being as much as possible.

FIGURE OUT WHAT WORKS FOR YOU

Think about your preferred way of being: Quick Start, Fact Finder, Follow Thru, or Implementor. How often are you able to be that way—in your job or at home? How does this alignment, or lack of alignment, support or discourage your efforts for doing better by the environment?

Then, when it comes to your conversations with others, how are you showing up? Are you mostly avoiding, accommodating, compromising, competing, or collaborating? Is this working? Test the conversational capacity skills out and see what works for you.

FIND YOUR RHYTHM

Work on reconnecting with your preferred way of being, and being with others, this week. Then, instead of doing a swap, incorporate your preferred way of being, and being with others, into your sustainability habits. If you are up for the challenge of taking on more swaps, check out the table at the end of the book for some ideas.

- Take the Kolbe A Index test, or if you choose not to spend the money, use the information on their website (www.kolbe.com) to guess your type. Identify changes you can make to live in a way more consistent with your natural state of being.

- Take the Thomas-Kilmann Instrument to determine your conflict management profile, or if you choose not to spend the money, use the information here to guess your profile. Identify conflict styles you are overusing or underusing and practice these styles.

- Figure out what type of sustainability activity makes you happy based on your type, and do it, or at least take the first step in making it happen. If this creates conflict at home (or work), assess your conflict management mode and see what you might do differently to get to collaboration.

Now imagine a workplace where in addition to building a diverse and inclusive culture based on how people look or dress or worship or love, the culture was also based on how people like to *be*, and how they can *be* better, together! Imagine if we understood how we each manage conflict and could integrate that into our workplace style. We could create the ultimate diverse and inclusive workplace culture.

Imagine if we applied all of this to finding our preferred way of doing better by the environment, and we were also able to influence others to do better, too!

Be . . . so you can spend! If you align your actions with your natural way of being, you can be intentional in how you spend your time and your money.

WEEK 4: SPEND

"If time is money, how much is a lifetime?"

– Ljupka Cvetanova, *The New Land*

From a money perspective, the average American spends almost twice as much on taxes as they do on savings. In other words, we give more, a lot more, to the government than we keep for ourselves. We are big spenders and have a low savings rate; more than a quarter of us have no emergency fund.[30]

From a time perspective, the typical American spends most of their waking hours interacting with electronic media, including more than a quarter of that time on television.[31]

What would happen if we got that money back? If we got that time back? What could we make room for?

Maybe you're struggling with feeling like the American dream is out of reach. When we ask, "How do I have it all?" we're asking the wrong question. It's not about having it all, it's about having enough. And knowing the answer to the question: what is your enough? Without answering that question clearly and concisely, we will keep spending—money and time—thoughtlessly.

Instead, if we *spend* intentionally we can *invest* intentionally. Spend (money and time) as little as possible on things you don't care about so you can invest (money and time) in the things you do care about. And if the environment is one of those things you care about, this intentionality can help get you where you want to go.

Thankfully, the lessons I learned about money—whether negative or positive—I was ultimately able to turn into something valuable. Not so much unraveling is required for these stories. It has been more about accepting them as okay.

MAKE CREDIT WORK FOR YOU

When I first started working after college, it only took a few years to accumulate a lot of credit card debt. I went from having no money to a decent salary and loved the freedom of spending it. To replace the $450 beater car my dad had bought for me in college—it had baling wire to hold the hood down—I bought a new (used) car as soon as I could. Within about five years, I bought a house and furnished it. I easily and happily fell into the trap of living large on credit. At some point, I came to my senses and paid off all of the credit card debt, and now I use credit cards very intentionally so that the credit card companies pay me. The monthly payments are set to auto-pay so we never miss a payment, which allows us to have excellent credit scores, and this system of making one big payment each month helps us manage cash flow.

We use credit cards for everything we possibly can and then use the accumulated points to travel to Denmark every summer to visit family. We scrupulously avoid bank fees of any kind.

However, this system does not work for everyone. Some families have systems where they pay in cash only. It helps them know exactly where their money goes, and they feel every expense, finding it makes them more intentional about their spending. I get it. Every quarter when we write the estimated income tax payment to the Internal Revenue Service (IRS), we feel it. When it comes out of a salary, many consider the money gone and forget about it. However you spend it—cash, check, debit, or credit—know where it goes.

FINANCIAL ADVERSITY CAN FOCUS US

We accumulated a lot of debt in 2017 during our perfect storm of me being out of commission due to the c-word, many medical bills, and a downturn in both of our industries (the energy and shipping markets). We also "save until it hurts" because of the tax advantages of making the largest allowed contributions to retirement funds for small businesses.

While we were never in danger of foreclosure or anything as challenging as what many other families faced, we went on an austerity program, looking hard at our expenses and making it so we could survive on a single income. I sustained the environmental habits already in place but was not in a mindset to take on any more challenges.

2019 was a much better year, and we are nearly debt free once again. That austerity program helped us get intentional about our spending.

The silver lining to financial adversity is that it helps us get focused on the difference between needs and wants. If we can carry those intentional spending habits with us during better times, then we will have more success in creating a path to a financially secure future.

INTENTIONAL SPENDING

I love Jean Chatzky and the *HerMoney* podcast. When I discovered her podcast, I binge-listened to every episode that was available and shared it with everyone I thought might be interested—or might need to hear it—man or woman, girl or boy. Jean talks about her fellow financial femme fatales Sallie Krawcheck and Suze Orman and the trope that if you took all the money you spent on café coffee every morning and instead saved that money, you would have a million dollars over a lifetime. Jean expressed it best when she said, "The f—ing latte is a f—ing metaphor."[32] If you want to buy coffee every day, do it, and do it intentionally and mindfully. Enjoy it!

I don't drink coffee, but I get the message. Even though I work from home, I frequently eat out for lunch. It would be easy to pounce on that and say, "Aha! Here is your chance to cut out an unnecessary expense." That $10 per day at five days a week for fifty weeks of the year will save you $2,500, which compounded annually will result in you having $X dollars in Y years (pick your amount).

Unfortunately, this kind of analysis just makes us feel bad and even if we stop the habit, the money just goes somewhere else. I choose to eat out most days at lunch because I enjoy vegetarian foods and it is hard to have both variety and freshness at home (without a lot of waste), not to mention that I live in a family of carnivores. It also helps me to get out from behind my desk and into the world as a mental and physical break during the workday. I try to make this my main meal of the day so that I can eat less in the evening when it is more likely to stick. And after all, we do need to eat. But maybe that just doesn't make sense to you and you enjoy cooking, you're good at it, or you like leftovers and taking them to work is not an issue. You'd rather have the money. Excellent! That is a choice, and as long as you are living within your means, there is no wrong choice here—make sure it is a choice and not something that just happens.

If you enjoy being thrifty, even better. Since I grew up feeling like we didn't have enough (although we actually did), I have been very intentional over the years about investing our money. But I don't like to be on a budget. It feels too much like when I was a kid and there often was no money available for things I wanted.

But some kids who grow up with thrifty parents become thrifty themselves. When my daughter and her friend were about ten or eleven years old, I asked for their help in creating Christmas goodie bags and selecting holiday-inspired gift cards for the fifteen teenage boys at a local residential treatment center. In addition to the gift card, I asked the girls to pick out $5 worth of candy for each boy's treat bag. My daughter was all in, but her friend was extremely selective about what she chose and carefully did the math on each item. She explained her choices, indicating that this one package had fifteen Pixy Stix for $1 so that would be a good purchase. It took a minute, but I finally understood that she was very carefully selecting candy items totaling $5 to cover all fifteen boys. She had not complained at all that this was too small an amount to work with and was doing her best to get the most for her money! We still laugh about it, but really, kudos to her thrifty parents.

It is only when we spend intentionally that we have money

left to invest—in our financial future and the things that are most important to us.

Spending money intentionally can help us get rid of stuff we never really needed anyway and can have the added benefit of helping us spend our time more intentionally as well. If you're not buying things, you're not spending time ordering them, tracking them, paying for them, unpacking them, disposing of the packaging, and figuring out what to do with them when they have reached the end of their useful life.

> Spending intentionally inherently
> helps the environment.

INTENTIONAL TIME MANAGEMENT

When you have kids and both parents work full time and commute to their jobs, it can seem like there just aren't enough hours in the day. Add in single parenting, ailing parents, financial worries, and medical issues and the situation can be overwhelming.

Research says we are only productive about three hours a day out of an eight-hour office day, yet people spend almost nine hours a day at work, not including the commute. The typical working adult in America spends the rest of the time reading news websites, checking social media, chitchatting with colleagues, looking for new jobs, taking smoke breaks, getting food and drinks, and so on.[33] Add in unproductive meetings, town halls, performance appraisals, training, emergencies, and computer updates and technology issues and it's no wonder companies hire consultants to actually get work done.

Every few years I go back and read or listen to Stephen R. Covey's 1990 book *The 7 Habits of Highly Effective People*.[34] The time management matrix Covey describes in "Put First Things First" has four quadrants categorizing activities as urgent or not urgent and important or not important. The important and urgent usually gets our attention (for example, getting to work, packing lunches for kids, getting kids to school). Most of us spend far too much time on the not important whether urgent or not urgent (e.g., social media, television), and not nearly enough time on the important but not urgent (e.g., developing a financial plan). If we spend less time on the not important things then we will have plenty of time to invest in the important things.

Having lived through having preschool-age children while working and commuting full time, I can vouch for the fact that no matter how good you are at practicing Covey's principles, there is still a very good chance that you will end up sleep deprived. And in a world without sufficient sleep, there is little room for anything perceived as extra—including worrying about recycling or using an alternative to plastic straws or plastic shopping bags. So what's the answer?

One of the greatest benefits of the remote work, freelance, gig economy we live in today is that we can get some of that time back. If you can find a way to work remotely even part of the time, or go independent, do it. For us, it was possible for me to take the leap to independent consulting because my husband had a full-time position that provided health insurance. When he also went out on his own (after seeing the flexibility I had and having his own personal last straw at work), our kids were seven and ten years old. We confronted the specter that is private health insurance and factored a high-deductible plan with a health savings account into our finances and are still with that plan today. You can place a number on every benefit that you are trading into or out of and determine whether you can make a financial go of it.

Now I routinely experience that state of flow that comes with working in a mostly uninterrupted focus on my work. I have shut off notifications for social media and messaging, and occasionally even shut off email—although not often, as a client calling is a client to be served. I have even been known to take a short nap when my productivity falls, or to take a walk to get an energy boost. I do things when it makes sense to do them. There is no implied pressure to put in "face time" and I have the flexibility to attend to important matters that aren't necessarily urgent. Of course, I also have the flexibility of working late, or working on the weekends when required!

It is only when we spend our time intentionally that we invest our time in the things most important to us.

Spend money and time intentionally.

FIGURE OUT WHAT WORKS FOR YOU

Figure out the money habits that work for you—credit cards or cash, electronic or paper. Just make sure that whatever method you use, you know where your money is going. Ask for help from a financial planner if it seems overwhelming.

Figure out the time habits that work for you as well. You may not be in a position to go solo, but you may be able to have a conversation with your employer about remote working days, flexible working times, or shortened workweeks. Think about getting a side gig going that will allow you to one day make the leap when the time is right. And if you are unable to make a change, avoid the traps that everyone else falls into and be as productive as you can during normal work hours so you can get out on time and beat the traffic. Forget about face time and don't apologize for not spending long hours at the office: your productivity and accomplishments will speak for themselves. And when you are off, detach from work and make time to sleep and play and be!

FIND YOUR RHYTHM

If you *spend* (mindlessly) as little time and money as possible, you will be able to *invest* (mindfully) as much time and money as possible. Then put sustainability into action by actually saving money (or time) while helping the environment

> For You

Take a look at your credit card or debit card or cash and check transactions for the last month. If you can't find the information, then track where your money goes for at least a week (a month is better). If you can find the information, then look through it for purchases that give you that bad feeling in your gut—because you don't even remember spending the money or are not using the thing you bought. Cut those out. It really is that simple.

After all, nobody deserves to feel bad about spending their own money.

Track your time for one week—divide it into the following categories: sleep, play, paid work, transport, household chores (laundry, cleaning, lawn care), acts of daily living (preparing, eating, and cleaning up from dinner, getting ready in the morning, or preparing for bedtime at night), kid stuff, activities you want to do (this could be dining out, watching movies, reading for pleasure, or something else you enjoy). Are you happy with the results? If not, what can you change?

> For the Environment

Make one change that saves money and also helps the environment (this is more or less the definition of sustainability). For example, change your electrical provider to one that is cheaper *and* provides a greater percentage of renewables, use ride sharing services, drive instead of fly, use washcloths instead of makeup wipes, plant wildflower seeds for pollinators instead of buying decorative plants at a nursery. Make up a practice that resonates with you.

Because we have had enough sleep, we have made time to play, we know how we like to be, and we are spending both money and time intentionally, we will have time to invest in the environmental goals we set for ourselves.

Spend . . . so you can serve! If you are spending your money and your time intentionally, you will have money and time to invest in service.

WEEK 5: SERVE

"The best way to find yourself is to lose yourself in
the service of others."

– Mahatma Gandhi

Approximately sixty-three million Americans, 25 percent of
the adult population, volunteer their time, talents, and energy,
according to nonprofitsource.com. On average, people spend
an about an hour a week volunteering, with the top four volunteer
areas being related to religion, education, social service, and health.

SERVING OTHERS IS GOOD FOR YOU

According to Dr. Jeanne Segal and Lawrence Robinson, there
are multiple ways that volunteering can make us "feel healthier
and happier" by connecting with others, engaging our mind
and body, and bringing fun and fulfillment into our lives.[35]
According to Dr. Segal:

- Serving others provides a counterbalance to negative emotions like anxiety and stress. Connecting with people and animals can have a real and positive impact on our mental health.

- Serving others can help fight depression. Maintaining routine connections with others can help us develop a network of support—both for us and for others— that can help reduce depression.

- Serving others can make us feel more confident and give us purpose. When we contribute to others, we feel like our efforts have value and we move our thoughts away from our own situation. We have a more positive outlook on life in general.

- Serving others keeps us moving. When we are active, we have better physical and mental health.[36]

The science says that our body releases endorphins when we donate money to charity, for example, and researchers have found that volunteers tend to live longer.[37] Sign me up!

CREATE A CULTURE OF SERVICE IN YOUR FAMILY

Without directly trying, we have created a culture of service in our family. I only just now realized that is what we have been doing these last twenty plus years as we raised our two children to (almost) adulthood.

Each of us volunteer in a capacity that aligns with our natural way of being. My Implementor husband and daughter "do," my Fact Finder son helps others through games, and my Quick Start self likes variety. See if any of these service examples give you ideas on how to serve.

My husband, Lars, bicycles from Houston to Austin each year in April to raise money for the National Multiple Sclerosis (MS) Society. Thanks to the generous support of his sponsors, he has even earned an engraving of his name on the walls at the MS Society office in Houston along with other top fundraisers.

A friend and I led our daughters' Girl Scouts troop for a few years. As the girls entered high school, our troop tried different types of service activities in our community, landing at Reining Strength Therapeutic Horsemanship for a project. The girls trained as side walkers and horse leaders, and helped during riding lessons for special needs kids. Kaitlin went there for the horses but fell in love with the kids. I would drop off a grumpy fifteen year old and pick up my happy, chatty, effusive daughter. Fast forward four years and she has completed her international certification as a therapeutic riding instructor at nineteen and is working with these very special riders. She tells wonderful stories of their successes, and I can see how good it makes her feel to be a part of their journey.

My son enjoyed volunteering at the county recycling center

during high school to earn a service cord. Now that he has graduated from college and is in the process of finding a job, he spends time each week playing board games with teenage boys at a nearby group home.

My penchant is advocating for those who cannot advocate for themselves—locally or across the ocean. Children deserve a voice. Because I was raising my own kids, I held off a bit until I felt I could devote the time and energy necessary. I dipped my toe in by becoming a surrogate parent at the local school. Surrogate parents do not do much in this context; mostly they sign the paperwork for assessment review meetings where the parents would sign if they were in the picture. At least I am supporting the everyday heroes and sheroes—the educators, diagnosticians, counselors, and coaches that help all our kids every day of the school year.

When my youngest reached middle school age and I felt like I could expand my role as a child advocate, I became a Court Appointed Special Advocate (CASA) or guardian ad litem for kids in the care of children's protective services. Our county program has a CASA appointed to each child (or family of children) in the care of the county. My first case lasted eighteen months and watching that child grow into a happy, healthy, secure home has been a joyous process. My second charge started as a "courtesy" or unofficial CASA case, as they were from a county outside my own. In time, I was able to be appointed by that county as a permanent CASA. That child has since reached the age of independence, so I am not sure whether or not our paths will cross again.

In the meantime, I have continued to serve as a surrogate parent for several teenagers in need. As wards of the state, these kids have been in and out of various placements and face a variety of challenges. I am able to visit them at the center where they live as well as participate in their school meetings. At least it provides some continuity for them and the school staff that provides services to them on a daily basis. During this process, I have seen what kind of documentation arrives with these students when they transfer in to our school district: as little as none, or at best, unclear or outdated records. We are fortunate to have professionals that make sure everything is done to support these students during their time in our community.

To be candid, it is often depressing to see the situations these kids come from and the challenges they face. It seems like an avalanche of difficulties: incarcerated, mentally ill, deceased, or intellectually disabled parents; physical, verbal, emotional, and sexual abuse; abandonment, neglect, and malnutrition. It's as though there are two planes of reality—the one we, the fortunate, live in and the one these kids live in—and the two planes never intersect.

While it can seem like these kids have largely been forgotten, they are in a safe and secure environment, with plenty of good food, shelter, medical care, and the structure that comes with regular school attendance. They also have their Children's Protective Services caseworker and group home staff, who are as kind and caring as they come, doing the best they can with the meager funds the state provides, and the educators who have dedicated their lives to supporting them.

Find your way to serve.

FIGURE OUT WHAT WORKS FOR YOU

You might serve through activities for a cause, with your children, through your church, or you might even create your own charity.

The church in many ways is a big part of the fabric that holds America together. If your volunteer place of choice is in the church, you are in good company; religious organizations use lots of volunteers.[38] Church communities have risen time and again to fill the gaps when the government cannot—during natural disasters, for the homeless, for immigrants. During Hurricane Harvey, the Red Cross served many meals to those rebuilding their lives and homes after the flood, and so did a group of Mennonites.

Recently I met two individuals who have managed their time, influence, and money for extraordinary service.

Celebrity Chef Jeff Henderson turned his life around and went from drug dealing and prison to chef, author, and speaker (www.chefjefflive.com). Chef Jeff works with kids in the prison system and has a charity that plants trees outside the windows of the cells where these children are incarcerated. The kids water "their" trees twice each day, watch them grow, and then harvest the fruit—learning to be responsible for another living thing and seeing a little bit of hope outside their window.

Another acquaintance also decided to create a charitable organization, Friday Harbour (www.fridayharbour.org), to address the lodging needs for people traveling to the Texas Medical Center in Houston for consultation or treatment. For one to three nights, Friday Harbour arranges for and covers the cost of the hotel stay. The process is seamless so these families have one less thing to worry about and can focus all of their attention on their loved one in care.

We can find service opportunities, or we can create them.

Big or little, service is integral to creating balance in our lives.

FIND YOUR RHYTHM

Take that newfound time (or money) and serve in a way that aligns with your preferred way of being.

> For You

What service are you called to? How can you make time for it—perhaps capitalizing on an existing part of your life (church), or including your children (4-H, Girl Scouts or Boy Scouts), or a passion or interest (pet shelters)? Think it through, see what your obligations allow, and then commit to a regular time, or as fits your schedule. See the world through the lens of whomever you are helping or serving. Embrace the endorphin release!

> For the Environment

Find an environmental or sustainability service opportunity that appeals to you and donate money or time. My favorites are Master Naturalists and the Nature Conservancy.

Whatever type of service you can fit into your schedule, I promise you will get as much from it as you give, probably more.

Serve . . . so you can shed! Once you reach out to help others, whatever burdens you might be carrying will be put into perspective and you can shed the made-up stories that are holding you back.

WEEK 6: SHED

"We were free of self-judgment when we were babies, and yet at some point, we developed a sensitivity that taught us to react with self-consciousness and negative self-talk."

– Elaina Marie, *Happiness Is Overrated - Live the Inspired Life Instead*

There is actual data that tells us people pay about half as much attention to us as we think they do.[39] So why do we care so much? Sometimes, you have to quit caring. Just a little bit. Or maybe a lot. Other times, you need to not have much in the way of expectations. That philosophy is allowing me to do something big at least for me, like publishing this book.

I can say in full confidence in the light of day when I am fresh from a restful night of sleep that I do not care how this book is received; I am doing it for me. Period. End of story. And yet. In the evening, as I wind down in the darkness that comes with the night, I have doubts. So many doubts. Most of them concluding with the question: Who do I think I am, daring to write a book?

So in the process of publishing this book, I am shedding my learned self-consciousness and negative self-talk.

LETTING GO OF THE STORIES WE TELL OURSELVES

For a lifetime, from childhood and through my career, I have been working on shedding the feeling that I need to conform to the standards that come from being a girl from a small farm town. We all have some self-limiting story we tell ourselves, based on the lessons of our lives.

Negative associations like these are taking up valuable space in our brains and we need to acknowledge the hurt, be grateful for whatever self-knowledge this pain has provided, and let them go. It's like I told my kids when they would have problems with a playmate: When it's good, let it be good. When it's not, turn away.

Sometimes, in these days of rampant social media, we feel bombarded with other people's stories. As a result, we might feel less than, not enough, or even bad when we compare our situation to that of others. We have to remind ourselves that most of these stories are not indicative of the real world.

Just like we turn away from those stories, we can learn to turn away from environmental habits that are not working and, as the next section tells us, even learn something about how to recycle in the real world.

SAY NO TO ASPIRATIONAL RECYCLING

We've all seen the Facebook posts of a charmed life (perfect children, perfect spouse, perfect life), even while knowing in reality it's just not so (the kids and spouse aren't so perfect, and neither is the life). I think of these as aspirational posts—they don't present how it really is, but rather how we would like it to be. We are wishing it so.

While we can accept that our Facebook friends present the life they aspire to, we should not accept aspirational recycling. Aspirational recycling, which is setting aside materials for recycling that cannot actually be recycled, is keeping us in a cycle of thinking of plastic as recyclable instead of separating it from our lives.

A shocking nine percent of all plastic ever made has likely been recycled, according to a global study cited by the National Geographic Society.[40] Close to 80 percent is stored in landfills or is breaking down in the environment as litter. Much of it will make its way to the oceans.

Items like soft plastics, Styrofoam, and wrapping paper are often unable to be recycled, or at least not without great effort. If we keep tossing them in the recycling bin, ever hopeful, we keep ourselves from tackling the real challenge of finding alternatives to produce bags and plastic-packaged items; as a result, we jam up the recycling centers machinery and potentially contaminate their product (plastic and paper) for reuse.[41]

It's time to let go of aspirational recycling and start finding alternatives to throw-away plastics. And while we're at it, let's reinforce the lessons we learned in Week 4 on how we spend time and money, by speaking about time and money intentionally as well.

IF YOU CAN'T SHED IT, REFRAME IT

There are words that evoke a gut reaction that makes me turn away from them; words like *budget, exercise, routine*. Budgets are constraining, exercise is a chore, and routine is boring. When I reframe the ideas each of those words represent, I can easily work them into my life:

I hate being on a budget. But I enjoy spending mindfully.

I hate exercise. But I enjoy physical activity.

I hate routine. But I love getting into a rhythm.

So if you really do need that budget, exercise, routine, or other thing that you keep turning away from, then don't shed it. Reframe it in a way that works for you and embrace it.

Likewise if recycling is a chore, reframe it as a challenge for how little trash you can generate. If composting is gross, reframe it as a neat experiment to see how natural decomposition works. If finding alternatives to plastic-packaged items is too difficult, reframe it as a game. You get the idea. It always seems to come back to the stories we tell ourselves, and we get to decide what those are.

THE WAY WE SPEAK ABOUT TIME AND MONEY

Along with our aspirational recycling, we can also shed these two expressions from our vocabulary: I don't have time. I don't have the money.

If we are intentional about how we spend our money and our time, then we do have the time for what is important to us and we do have the money for what we need.

Wouldn't it be more accurate to say, this isn't a priority for me right now, or yes, we have the money, and that's not how we choose to spend it?

This is an important conversation to have with the young people in our lives.

How we spend our time reveals our priorities, and if we don't model that for our kids, how will they learn what good time management looks like? My kids know to find me at my desk (usually) if they need me. I used to feel bad about it, looking like I was working all the time. Then I realized that I was both modeling a strong work ethic and was still available whenever my kids needed.

Likewise, how we spend our money reveals our priorities. If

the response to every request is we don't have the money, the kids will know that is not true when they see you spend money at the grocery store or on other necessities or on the stuff you want but not what they want. If we instead say we have just enough money for groceries but no extra, then we will help our kids understand the differences between needs and wants.

The way we speak about money and time is based on the way we feel about money and time.

THE WAY WE FEEL ABOUT MONEY

Why are our feelings about money, like having enough or not having enough or what is enough, so complicated? How have the lessons we have learned and the stories we have told ourselves over the course of our lives conspired to create our current financial situation—good or bad? And how we can let go of whatever might be making us feel bad about it?

Sallie Krawcheck, the CEO and cofounder of Ellevest, gave me permission to be my authentic self when it came to finances. Self-taught through voracious reading and trial and error, I have guided our family finances into providing college educations for our children, investments in land, and a comfortable retirement for my husband and me. I fretted that I checked my finances too frequently—daily in fact. Jean Chatzkey says you're not supposed to do that. What was wrong with me that I needed this daily assurance that our money was there? The conventional wisdom is to check infrequently or set it and forget it, lest you succumb to the emotions of market volatility and be tempted to invest high and sell low.

Sallie shared that she grew up feeling financially insecure and thus obsessed (my word, not hers) over her finances. Hearing a very successful woman like Sallie say this made me accept my penchant for running the numbers to see exactly where we stand every weekday. It is one of the signals that the workday has ended for me. I felt financially insecure as a child as well and checking our finances each day gives me a sense of security.

Although our family was not actually financially insecure, money was a source of strife between my parents. I vowed never to be financially dependent on anyone so that I could always choose to be with someone and not be trapped. I never felt like I had enough clothing to avoid wearing the same outfits at school during the week (plus I am tall so pants that were long enough were hard to find). References to "selling a pig" in the fall to get school clothes contributed to a feeling of not having enough.

My parents did better by their children than their parents did by them (as did their parents before them), and we had many opportunities that my parents did not. Having a safe, secure, stable childhood was the greatest gift I was ever given, and I only learned to appreciate that privilege as an adult. (None of my siblings have indicated that same financially insecure feeling. In fact, my younger sister shared once that my ability to manage money made her feel inferior! Oh, the stories we tell ourselves.)

Just like we all have a play history, we have a money history, and it is either working for us or it is working against us.

THE WAY WE FEEL ABOUT TIME

We probably have a time story, too. Mine is that moms and dads didn't have time to play because they worked. They worked all day at a job, and they worked in the evenings on the farm or in the vegetable garden. This is great for modeling work ethic, but not so great for modeling play. I was never great at playing with my own kids. Everything had to have a purpose: educational (reading stories at bedtime) or service oriented (volunteering for service cord hours or college application material). I can see now that there was a real missed opportunity there. If I could go back, I would work harder at playing with my kids.

How we spend our time will model our priorities for our children and others in our lives. If we say we have no time for sleep, play, school, eating healthy, recycling—pick your issue—and then we spend a large part of our day on the computer and social media, our actions are not aligned with our priorities.

If we can shed these behaviors, we can be more intentional about our actions and choices, and hopefully, those we influence will follow.

THE WAY WE SPEAK ABOUT OURSELVES

When we let go of the negative stories about ourselves, and speak intentionally about time and money, we become free to speak about ourselves in positive and intentional ways. To that end, here are some other ways of being that we can shed:

- Being self-deprecating
- Staying in our lane
- Apologizing:
  - For having an idea
  - For being a leader
  - For being a follower
  - For being an independent thinker
- Being anything but your authentic self
- Feeling bad because your way of being doesn't conform to society's idea of how or who you should be

Craig Weber, mentioned in Week 3 on being, has a great discussion of our tendency to minimize ourselves in his book, *Conversational Capacity*.[42] We sacrifice our views when we have "a strong need to keep things comfortable, to avoid conflict, to keep things calm." We can end up falling into the trap of not speaking up when we should, not saying anything (which can be taken as agreement), or watering down what we need to say. We might even discuss the matter behind their back rather than expressing our points of view, which may really need to be expressed!

A few years back, my younger sister, Jenny, and I were collecting roofing materials for a shed from an Amish family contracting out of their home. As they loaded the materials from their barn, we could see the load would not be secure enough for the drive home. Jenny deferentially said something to the effect of, "You know, I really don't know much about this, my husband sent me to get these materials, but I am just wondering if we shouldn't stick these long pieces on here a different way." The men quietly adjusted the load and we were on our way.

While we were in the truck I asked her why she acted like she didn't know what she was doing when I knew she was perfectly capable of seeing the problem and resolving it. (Jenny is a doer. Kolbe would probably call her an Implementor.) At first, she didn't know what I was talking about. Then she realized that she was self-deprecating, diminishing her abilities to make the Amish father and son more comfortable, in case they might somehow be offended by taking direction from a woman when women in their households have different roles. The fact is, their demeanor was quiet and efficient, and there was no evidence they were uncomfortable dealing with women rather than men. Clearly, with the business they are in, they deal with individuals outside their religion all the time. So why do we as women feel like we have to present our abilities as diminished to avoid offending men? Can't we just be efficient, too, and carry on? Chances are that men are not offended, and we have just made that up in our heads. And if men are offended, well that's on them.

SHEDDING PLASTICS

Just like we can shed negative associations to make room for something better, we can shed many plastics from our life. We just don't need them; we never actually did. Take plastic straws, for example. In the US, we are using an estimated 500 million plastic straws *every day*. One study estimates that eight billion straws contaminate our planet's beaches.[43] Just like the latte metaphor in Week 4, plastic straws are a symbol for single-use plastics. Most of us just don't need them for everyday living. If we can shed our notions about what we think we need and replace them with mindful intentionality of what we really do need, we can get rid of the new (disposable plastics) and restore the old (reusable materials).

Shed negative self-talk and stories that
don't serve you.

FIGURE OUT WHAT WORKS FOR YOU

Only you know the stories, feelings, and expressions that are not working for you, so figure out what does work for you. Experiment and monitor the results. There is no right or wrong. It's a journey that will never have an end point, and that's okay.

FIND YOUR RHYTHM

Shed the things holding you back, and shed some single-use plastics, too, this week.

> For You

Identify one bit of negative self-talk. Now, shed it. Just let it go. It really is that simple. When it reappears, acknowledge it and then say goodbye. Replace it with something positive and remind yourself of that good thing every day this week. Start and end the day with that good thought. Make a note and tape it to your mirror or your car sun visor. Tell a friend and ask them to remind you. Whatever it takes!

> For the Environment

You're on a roll now! Here are more opportunities to swap this for that. Choose at least one single-use, plastic item and eliminate it from your life:

- Swap plastic disposable plates with cardboard disposable plates.
- Swap Styrofoam to-go containers with reusable containers you carry with you.
- Swap plastic cutlery with metal cutlery you carry with you.

Once we shed hopes not reflected in reality and expressions that aren't really true, we can work on shedding activities that are not important to us. Let's identify those activities and then reduce the amount of time and money we spend on them. Then take that newfound time and spend it on something important, like sleep or play or self-care or other important, but not necessarily urgent, things. We'll have time to create intentions around our shopping and recycling activities, too.

Shed . . . so you can stretch! When you have shed the non-essential in your life, you will have time to stretch and to grow.

WEEK 7: STRETCH

"Thank you adversity. Oh, how we stretch and grow in the shadows of darkness just to reach the light."

– Bryant McGill, *Simple Reminders: Inspiration for Living Your Best Life*

We all have had some kind of adversity in our lives—maybe many kinds of adversity, even all at once. We may not have a choice about the thing that happens to us, or to someone we love, but we have a choice about how that adversity shapes us. If we allow adversity to stretch us, we can extend ourselves to reach the light, and with light comes growth.

ONE OF MY ADVERSITY STORIES

May 15, 2017, was the day my hair fell out. It had been coming out in handfuls daily for about a week, but having a thick head of hair meant it wasn't noticeable to anyone but me. Until that day. It's ironic that I can't remember the exact day my doctor said I had a mass in my right breast, or the exact day of the surgery to remove it, or the exact day chemotherapy started, or the exact day I had to lay my bald, half-naked self out for radiation treatment the first time. But I remember the day my hair left my head so brutally and completely.

My oncologist told me it would, indeed, fall out. But I had continued to be hopeful that maybe *my* hair wouldn't fall out (part of my coping mechanism I called "plausible deniability"— more on that later). After all, I had a full head of wild hair when I was born; I was surely different. So I wasn't prepared when it did. No wig, no hat, no scarf, no disguise. I cried only twice through the whole ordeal. This was the second time, standing in the shower, holding all my hair, so much hair, and then stepping out and stuffing it in the wastebasket. (The first time was realizing, in the doctor's office, that I was going to have to tell my eighty-something-year-old mom, who had experienced so much loss, that her daughter had breast cancer.)

I called MD Anderson Cancer Center's beauty parlor as soon as they opened, but no one answered. I pulled what few strands of my shoulder-length hair were left into a sad ponytail, trying not to look into the mirror at the exposed scalp, then I made the drive into the city. I parked and walked as fast as I could through the endless maze, past elevators A and B and C and D and E and into infinity it seemed, conscious that all eyes were on me—although of course, they weren't. If you're at MD Anderson on a Monday morning, you have your own problems. I finally arrived and—they were closed. No reason. Nothing on the phone voicemail greeting. Just closed.

Nearly in tears, I made the humiliating journey back to my car and pulled out the portfolio where I kept all my cancer patient papers and found the list of wig providers for people like me. I called until I found one that was open, and they were very kind. I made a quick decision on the first shoulder-length wig that I found, called my sister so we could FaceTime to get her opinion, and then was set to go out into public. My very kind hairstylist made a house call to shave off the remaining wisps so that I did not have to share my situation.

Sometimes we stretch ourselves, and sometimes life does the stretching for us. Either way, we get to decide what to do with that stretch.

WE GET TO DECIDE HOW TO HANDLE IT

I never asked, "Why me?" I'm more of a "Well, why not me?" kind of person. One in eight women in the US will develop breast cancer over the course of a lifetime.[44] So, I am hardly the only member of this unfortunate club. Many have had a much worse experience than mine.

And as many people as there are in this world, there are as

many ways of dealing with adversity. It was so painful to me to tell those who I cared about, and who cared about me, that I had cancer—a very charged, very scary word. I had to limit the number of times I did that in order to have the energy to care for myself. I truly hope that all the people that I didn't tell, who felt like they should have been let in, will get that it has nothing to do with how I feel about them and everything to do with caring for myself. Plus it's so boring to talk about! Whatever else there is to talk about, that is better, more interesting. If we can choose between *this* (c-word) and *that* (anything else), *that* is always better!

Under my approach of plausible deniability, you don't deny the medical care we are so lucky to have in this country, but you pretend everything else is normal. You tell only those with a need to know, and as much as possible, you carry on with your normal schedule (aside from medical appointments and a lot of sleep).

So, I told as few people as possible that I had cancer and the ones I did tell were sworn to secrecy. To my mind, I didn't have cancer for very long—maybe six weeks from suspicion to confirmation to removal. It was discovered during a mammogram, and even when I was told it was there, I couldn't find it—dense breast tissue, it's a thing, apparently. At first, it was going to be a real non-event: Stage 1. Take it out, test the lymph nodes (they were clean), do some radiation, wrap it up, and call it a day. No one would ever need to know.

Then my oncologist recommended we send the tumor off for testing to determine the likelihood of recurrence using a test called Oncotype DX that looks at a specific set of markers on the tumor itself. Your tumor gets graded (shouldn't all tumors get an F for fail?!), a score for the markers it has. If it scores in the upper third, you need chemo. If it falls in the lower third, chemo will not do any good. If the score falls in the middle—can't say chemo will help, can't say it won't. Of course, mine fell right smack dab in the middle of the middle. I know myself and I am not good with regret, so I went ahead with the chemo. I'll never know if it made a difference. If the dreaded c-word doesn't come back, maybe it never would have. If it does, it probably would have anyway.

So really, the cancer didn't make me sick, it was the preventive medicine. And because it was not to treat the cancer but to prevent a recurrence, I did not get the worst of the chemo. Four times, three weeks apart, two kinds of intravenous drugs, plus a steroid and anti-nausea medication. After that, two weeks of radiation, five days a week and done. It still sucks. Let's hope for a day when we don't have to make people sick to get them well or to prevent them from becoming sick.

Even though I wasn't totally embracing the sustainability thing at that point in my life, I did see so many opportunities at MD Anderson for recycling plastic cups used at the water dispensers, and separating trash from recycling. I never did bring it up—when someone is fighting for their life, recycling is pretty low on the totem pole of priorities.

This kind of decision-making—which initiatives to launch and which to let go of—is part of deciding how we handle our sustainability efforts, based on what else is going on in our life.

FINDING HUMOR IN ADVERSITY MAKES IT BEARABLE

As with any adversity, there are also humorous moments. While talking with a breast reconstructive surgeon, I was told with regard to "the girls," that they are sisters, not twins—as a preface to letting me know that one of my girls was smaller than the other. And of course, the one they had to remove the small, lemon-sized tissue and tumor from was the smaller of the girls.

The surgeons did amazing work. The oncology surgeon removed the tumor and a safety margin of tissue around it. Then while I was still out, the reconstructive surgeon came in and through the same incision, separated the underlying tissue from the overlying layer of skin and smushed it all about to fill in the hole. I am a cup size smaller on that side, but when I notice in photos, I just pretend it's the camera angle. I can still get additional reconstructive surgery done to get closer to having twins. We'll see if that ever happens; every time I have surgery, I vow it to be the last time.

I had a little bit of fun with the wig, too. Under my plausible deniability approach, I had to decide who I really *had* to tell. My CASA kid was in the hospital for emergency surgery, so I visited him daily and got to know the caretakers that stayed with him. One day I had my hair, and the next day I had a wig. I did not say a word about it. The last thing I wanted to do was to add to this kid's load by mentioning me in combination with the c-word. Neither my CASA kid nor his caretaker said a peep. The caretaker told me later that after I left the first time with the wig, he asked my CASA kid if he noticed my hair. They both had but did not say anything. Thank you, gentlemen. I appreciate it.

During my bald days, I had a dear cousin in the hospital and had to decide: Do I stop reaching out to family in need because I don't want to tell them about the cancer? I took my chances and visited Amy and she told me how much she liked my new hairstyle. Her mom and her daughter arrived, and apparently, this wig was styled better than my own hair because I kept getting compliments. Then my great aunt arrived, Amy's grandmother, who is known for being rather forthright. She informed me that she didn't like it at all. She liked my old style better because this one was too perfect (and if you know me, you know the only time my hair is perfect is when I walk out of the hair salon). But nobody thought it was a wig! You have to love family that likes the imperfect you best.

When life stretches us, finding the humor in the adversity can help us have the positive outlook needed to keep working on the sustainability habits that are important to us but are a stretch for our current energy level.

SOMETIMES ADVERSITY PILES ON

So once the radiation was complete and my treatment was done, there was more in store for us. It turned out 2017 was one of *those* years. You know the kind. You start out all optimistic, making plans to do great things—or at least to keep what you have going. Between my husband and I, we had: a double hernia repair (he had to get it done quickly so that he would be ready for my surgery), breast cancer (me), and a broken wrist (him— it's amazing what they can do with titanium). We quickly met our health insurance deductible, so I told my husband, "Guess what honey, you are due for your colonoscopy." And yes, they can do that procedure just a week after fixing a wrist; he had the same anesthesiologist for both procedures. It's so fun to get to know your health care professionals so well.

But all that we could have handled. We both work for ourselves, which means you can work whenever—and you do work whenever. We thought we were the best-diversified couple career-wise, with him in shipping and me in environmental consulting, but 2017 corrected that thinking. In the years immediately preceding, my company of one had grown to a team of six. For my husband, the shipping industry was going great guns, too. And then the bottom fell out of everything. Companies started closing, jobs became scarce, and profit margins fell.

One of my Houston-based energy clients closed an entire business line overnight, with our auditor still in the field. They were all cutting consultants and staff hard. We carry disability insurance, but it doesn't count the first ninety days of the disability and requires a lot of paperwork. I wonder how really sick people manage to get it all completed. And then, of course, processing time. But, it was better than nothing. So first the medical hit—both on our time and energy, but also our finances. Then my work dropped off, his work dropped off, and we were feeling it all.

We visit my husband's family in Denmark every summer and figured we just did not have the time, energy, or money to do it in the summer of 2017. We had made the decision, which meant we would not see his parents and brother for two years (2016 was the last visit). No one was happy about it. Lars was dreaming of breakfast on the patio in the Danish summer and Kaitlin was missing her horse-riding friends there. We were depressed, and I couldn't take it. I launched into "momma gonna make this happen" mode (all the mommas out there know what I am talking about). I got the exact day that my radiation protocol would end, and the exact date of my daughter's first day of eleventh grade, and we managed to squeeze in two weeks in Denmark, although without our son, Nic, who would be starting his third year at college at that time. My husband went over early to get everything ready (we have a summer house there), so that I would not have to help make up beds and get the house ready. This way I would be able to arrive and collapse into bed.

Kaitlin and I managed to get an entire middle row to ourselves on our British Airways flight. The wig can be very itchy and not conducive to sleep, so I pulled up the hood on my sweater and flopped the wig in the seat between us; it landed flat with the backside up and next to her jacket. Kaitlin tells me that while I was asleep, the flight attendant walked past, paused, looked at the middle seat, and in her British accent, her head cocked to one side, asked Kaitlin, "Is there an infant?" Kaitlin just said, "No," offering no explanation and enjoying the puzzled look on the attendant's face. If that was a child, then it could only have been a flattened baby Cousin It. I got a double take from the flight attendant when I walked off the plane with the hair of the small child on my head.

We got a much-needed break in Denmark. But the year had more in store for us. As our return day approached, we learned of a tropical storm—soon to become Hurricane Harvey—working its way through the Gulf of Mexico. It looks much worse when you are watching it from Europe than when you are monitoring it from Houston. We left Copenhagen on a Friday and arrived in Houston that evening to rainy but manageable weather. Our son was to pick us up, but the navigation took him to the wrong location. When we finally connected, we told him to get home and we would hire a car.

"By the way," he said, "I didn't have time to get groceries for the morning." When we got home, Lars and Nic went grocery shopping only to find the shelves of the first store they went to empty. They eventually cobbled together enough to stock us up. On Saturday morning, we got Nic back to College Station to make sure he would not get stranded at our home. Then we secured the house. By Sunday, we had our friends who knew their property would definitely flood staying with us. Their house had several feet of water in it during the 2016 floods so they razed it and built a new one four feet higher even though a three-foot elevation was all that was required (thank goodness because the floodwaters went more than three feet). They emptied their refrigerator and freezer, got their animals to safe places, and stayed with us from Sunday until Wednesday. We watched the creek behind us, we watched the weather news, we watched movies, we ate, we slept, we chewed our nails. And then we repeated it for three days.

We were very lucky. Our home never flooded, and the swimming pool and water well were safe. We had moved the rabbit from the bunny hutch and run that would have been submerged. The creek that borders our property was a raging river and although it was at least twice as high and twenty times as wide as it had ever been, we were never in danger. We had been tested, and we were safe. Our neighborhood was an island, but we were okay.

The greatest loss was a playhouse from when our daughter was young. We found it after the rain finally stopped and we were able to do a walkabout. It had floated about half a mile down the creek and lodged in between the trees of a home in the next neighborhood over (they asked to keep it). The biggest surprise was a yellow-bellied water snake trapped in the bunny run. Kaitlin's scream alerted us to it when she was starting to clean out all of the debris in the hutch area. The poor snake wanted out as bad as we wanted it out, but it couldn't find the exit because the bottom of the door opening was a foot off the ground. Eventually, we made a staircase out of bricks, left the door open and it was gone the next morning.

So many had been devastated by Hurricane Harvey (and even now, more than two years later, many are still recovering). The stories from our friends and families' narrow escapes are scary: some thought they were safe and stayed in their home with the water rapidly rising and the lights still on; others walked through waist-deep water for a mile, pushing a boat with their small cousin and dogs; another could rode an airboat out of a flooded house against strong currents with only one life jacket—for the dog.

The effects were widespread and overwhelming, and I desperately wanted to help, just as I had during the 2016 floods. But it took very little to exhaust me, and I was immunosuppressed from the chemo. My friend Lisa told me I was not to help with the cleanup. Period. I sat back and watched, sad that I could do little else. We didn't even have enough cash flow to donate money.

Hurricane Harvey capped an exhausting year, and thankfully, 2018 and 2019 were very boring.[45]

To be candid, this was one of the periods of my life when sustainability was not on my mind; I was just trying to sustain myself and my family. We maintained the status quo, but there was little room for any new initiatives.

It was only after things were well on their way to being back to normal that I had the energy to look at the world and my place in it through a new lens. After all, I was still here and I could still do. My attention and focus were more crystallized than ever, and I was intent on doing better for the environment.

The big takeaway from this time in my life was that sometimes we will work harder on our environmental initiatives than at other times, and that's okay. We may not be able to control everything that is going on in our lives, but if we focus on what we *can* do, then we will get a bit of that control back.

SMALL WINS MATTER

Two years later, my hair has grown back and like Samson of the biblical Samson and Delilah, my strength seems to correlate to my hair length. We faced adversity—cancer, financial issues, a hurricane—and we came through stronger. We continue to catch up from that time period, but the end is in sight. Every day, things get a little better. A kid graduates from college, another launches her career, we acquire new clients, we increase our physical activity and improve our eating habits. We also look for ways to remove waste from our lives: money waste, time waste, and waste to landfills, too.

Celebrating these small wins has helped build us back up. In the *Harvard Business Review,* authors Teresa Amabile and Steven J. Kramer talk about what they call "the progress principle." The one most important thing that can put us in a good place each day is making progress in meaningful work. The more we have those small wins, the more likely we are to make progress over time.[46]

As we move into the final weeks, I'll share how I translated adversity into stretch by using specific methods to create new habits and finding space for new ways of being and thinking.

Stretch yourself. Only you know what
that looks like.

FIGURE OUT WHAT WORKS FOR YOU

Sometimes we stretch ourselves, and sometimes life events apply the stretch for us. Find humor where you can and take energy from it. Focus on what is within your control—what you *can* do. Give yourself a break if your focus on environmental initiatives seems hit or miss sometimes.

No matter what is going on, acknowledge and celebrate the small wins that happen every day.

FIND YOUR RHYTHM

Work on figuring out your why, whether based in adversity or not. Then as long as we're thinking big, see if you can up your game and swap out something a little more challenging for something more sustainable.

> For You

What is your stretch? What is your why? Map out a how (a plan). Now do it, or at least set the wheels in motion. Celebrate the small wins. Accept the setbacks. Carry on. Share your stretch ideas with a friend.

> For the Environment

You've got this now, so we're moving on to some bigger challenges. Choose an item from the following (or make something up yourself) and stretch yourself in eliminating a single-use plastic that is challenging you:

- Swap disposable razors for metal reusable razors.
- Swap plastic flossers or pics for wooden toothpicks.
- Swap single use plastic lighters for long wooden matchsticks.
- Swap plastic disposable diapers with a cloth diaper service.

Maybe you have a big stretch story, maybe not. We all stretch or get stretched at some point in our lives. Focus on small wins to keep from getting overwhelmed, and always find gratitude for the things that *are* working in your life.

Stretch . . . and inhabit! When you stretch yourself, you will find you can inhabit a new rhythm with ease.

WEEK 8: INHABIT

"For years, home has been idealized as a refuge from the world, somewhere predictable and unchanging. But home isn't just where we go to escape the world. Home is how we inhabit the world. Meaning comes from connection and a willingness to pay attention to the particulars of our lives, from the things we choose to use to our daily rituals and shared activities."

– Louisa Thomsen Brits, *The Book of Hygge: The Danish Art of Living Well*

"Plastic will inhabit the oceans long after man has gone."

– Anthony T. Hincks

It is often said we are creatures of habit; we have our routines, our systems, our rhythms, the structure that forms the framework for the cadence of our lives. If our habits are our daily rituals, then they also inform how we inhabit the world.

Better habits, better health, better happiness, and better relationships lead to a better environment.

But creating new habits and breaking old ones is hard. It seems like the odds really are stacked against us. After all, it can take a long time to create a habit—ten weeks is average, but it could be much more. A lack of time, money, support, options—and a stack of health or relationship issues—can make it really hard to change our ways even when we know if we could, things would be better.

In this chapter, I share four ways you can work on incorporating sustainable habits into your life. Try them out, see what works for you, and you may even find yourself applying them to other aspects of your life.

MAKE IT EASIER

Ashley Whillans, a behavioral scientist at Harvard Business School, says the research tells us, "When people are feeling pressed for time, environmental actions that don't take very much time all of a sudden feel impossible—composting, recycling, remembering to turn off all the lights in your house before you leave."[47] This sounds like me when I really want to use a reusable bottle for water when I visit a client at their office but I forget to take it. Those plastic water bottles are just so easy to buy. They are in every store and kiosk. And then I can feel like, well, at least I recycle them when they are empty. In an interview with Whillans, NPR writer Ailsa Chang says this is called the "intention-action gap, which means you can care deeply about the environment and still fail to do things you know are good for the environment." Turns out, we need to make the thing that is good for the environment easier than—or at least as easy as—the thing that is not.

Little did I know, that is what I was doing when I changed out my dental floss. There was a time when I didn't floss every day. As a child, I would lie about having brushed my teeth. It is hard for me to understand that young mind because now I could never go to bed without brushing and flossing my teeth. It is a habit that is ingrained in me but at one time it was an interruption to what I considered the natural flow of allowing my sleepy little self to fall into bed. Now I wouldn't dream of going to bed without flossing. It's part of my nighttime routine and it takes no time at all; it is a habit that I inhabit. But, if it's not bad enough that conventional dental floss is one of those use-it-and-toss-it items made of synthetic material, there is also the potential for chemicals in or on the floss being absorbed into your body, not to mention the issue of the disposal of the used strings of polymer and the plastic floss holders.[48]

Of course, I'm going to floss my teeth every night. At least I don't use the plastic pick flossers. It seems like a small thing, but according to Jodi Breau, "for every person in the US who flosses their teeth according to ADA recommendations [in one year], just the empty floss dispensers alone would fill a landfill the size of a football field six stories high!"[49] Jodi is the creator of dental lace (www.dentallace.com), which is an alternative to synthetic floss and is made of compostable mulberry silk. It even comes in a refillable glass container with a stainless steel cap. I was a little worried about it being glass, but the small, cylindrical shape of the container seems to give it enough structure to travel well, tucked inside a corner of my makeup bag.

An avid composter (if avid means I put stuff on the compost and never touch it again), at first I was hesitant to actually compost the floss. But I got over the ick factor and now collect the used floss along with cotton balls (from applying toner) for composting in our outside collection area with fruit and vegetable matter from the kitchen, leaves, and fallen fruit and plant trimmings from the yard. So just be careful if you come to my house, and don't borrow a cotton ball from the jar on my vanity—you might be in for a surprise.

Using dental lace is actually easier because the lace never gets tangled or separated in the little wheel inside, unlike the conventional plastic floss dispenser, and I set up a subscription service to receive refills every few months. I never have to notice that it's about to run out, add it to my shopping list, remember to buy it at the store, or hurt myself opening a plastic-packaged multipack of plastic floss containers ever again! The refills have a smaller profile and are easier to store. Plus, I never have to wonder if the empty plastic containers are actually getting recycled, or if they are one of those aspirational items we put with the recyclables and hope they get recycled (but actually gets tossed in the trash, or worse, jams the machinery). And I never have to worry that an animal or bird rummaging through a landfill will become entangled in or choke on used floss. Yes, I think about those things.

MAKE IT CHEAPER

Another way to close the intervention-action gap is to make the green thing we want to do cheaper.[50] We finally found a waste disposal company that also does curbside, mixed-stream recycling, and they do it for just an additional ninety-two cents per month! They provide a separate bin and pick the bin up weekly just like the trash pickup service they also provide. Now, instead of sorting our recyclables and accumulating the materials in the garage to take to the county recycling center on a regular basis, we only need to go there every few months for items the company won't take—batteries, bulbs, aerosol cans. Cheap and easy!

Our home is all electric and even though electricity is deregulated in Texas, meaning we can choose where our power comes from (www.powertochoose.com), I am embarrassed to admit that I have always selected the cheapest provider (my dirty little secret). I always *look* at the providers of renewables, and if the cost is the same, I'll select the one with more renewables, but when it comes to clicking the link, it just seemed so expensive to choose the greener option. Finally last year, I found a 100 percent renewable provider at 8.7 cents per kilowatt-hour. That is less expensive than the other options with fewer or no renewables, so it was easy to make the decision when the cheapest option was also the greenest option. According to Ashley Whillans, the Harvard Business School behavioral scientist mentioned above, I am not alone. When trying to get people to choose a more sustainable option, financial incentives help.[51]

ASK FIVE WHYS

Forgetting my reusable water bottle when I visit a client is especially embarrassing since I am an environmental consultant, and also because one client, in particular, has managed to eliminate disposable cups except for spares tucked away for visitors. I don't have a specified place to put my things, so leaving a reusable mug doesn't work for me like it would for an employee. To help me on my quest to stop using water from plastic water bottles, I am borrowing the five whys method from the founder of the automotive manufacturer Toyota, Sakichi Toyoda. This system, used in many business improvement processes such as Lean and Six Sigma, goes like this: "When a problem occurs, ask 'why' five times in order to find the source of the problem, then put into place something to prevent the problem from recurring."[52] For my water bottle problem, I asked myself:

1. Why do I get to my client's office, only to realize I do not have anything to drink out of? *Because I forgot my reusable bottle (and they no longer offer disposable cups).*

2. Why did I forget my reusable bottle? *Because I didn't see it when I left the house, and for me, out of sight is out of mind.*

3. Why was it out of sight? *Because after I wash it, I put it away in the kitchen cabinet.*

4. Why do I put it away in the kitchen cabinet? *Because that is where we store coffee mugs.*

5. Why do I store it with the coffee mugs? *Because I wasn't thinking about how I need visual cues to remember things when I walk out the door.*

I'm storing my new water bottle in my car so I will always have it, but wouldn't you know, it's too tall to fit under the client's water dispenser. I know because I made a mess trying. I'll be on the lookout for a shorter version.

BUNDLE IT

Finally, Judson Brewer, in his article "How to Break up with Your Bad Habits," suggests analyzing habits you want to change by addressing the three parts of the habit—the trigger, the behavior, and the reward.[53] It is the reward that reinforces the behavior, so if we can harness that piece, we are more likely to succeed. In other words, we need to find something more rewarding than the reward of the behavior we want to change. This requires mindfulness that there is a reward at all. Get curious about why you do what you do, and when you have discovered that, you can substitute a different, better reward. It's kind of like another story you tell yourself, but a helpful one.

Like that good feeling I get when I pick up trash so that the kids playing in the neighborhood can take growing up in a nice, safe, and clean environment for granted. This goes right along with another technique to getting ourselves to do something we feel like we should do but don't want to do, or even dread. If we pair the dreaded thing with something we want to do but for some reason feel like we shouldn't, we are rewarding ourselves for accomplishing that dreaded thing.

Those who have studied this call it "bundling." I call it a dirt sandwich—stick one unpleasant thing between two good things or one unpleasant thing on top of one good thing (an open-faced dirt sandwich). An example given in the research pairs lunch with a person you don't really like but need to stay in touch with, with a favorite but unhealthy or expensive meal at a restaurant you really like but is more of a treat.[54]

So for me, the litter accumulating along the road outside our neighborhood disrupts the good feeling I have about living in the country. I really don't want to go out there and pick up trash. There's always more than you can see when you're driving. It's usually a dirty job because it has been there a while, and I never seem to bring enough bags. I just don't like being out there—I feel vulnerable. So when it's really bugging me (and the weather is cooler, to avoid snakes), I pair the activity of picking up the trash with walking for physical activity, listening to my favorite podcast and decompressing, and then later I can enjoy that satisfying feeling every time I pass by and see the clean fencerows and ditches.

GET THE KIDS INVOLVED

This is a great place to mention getting the kids involved. Habits started at a young age—good or bad—can last a lifetime. A perfect example of this relates to how food waste is managed in Denmark. In addition to the normal curbside recycling containers, each homeowner gets a small green box with a lid and handle, and special green bags to line it. All the kitchen and table scraps go in that box, and then when the bag is full, it is tied and placed in the designated curbside bin.

Kids are so used to collecting the table scraps at home that they get confused at school when there are no food waste boxes in the lunchroom. What are they supposed to do with the leftover bits from lunch? Of course, it just goes in the trash—but what an opportunity lost. I learned about this a couple years back; hopefully this gap has been addressed by now.

We had a similar routine when we were kids, but the table scraps went to the dogs, and it was our job to carry the vegetable and fruit waste to the hogs—the ultimate recyclers.

Whether it's a chore or a routine, or something you turn into a game, oftentimes kids have an easier time adopting sustainable systems and habits than adults.

Inhabit your habits.

FIGURE OUT WHAT WORKS FOR YOU

I applied the "make it easier" method for getting plastic straws out of my life. I only "need" a straw for drinks in the car, so I have stainless steel straws with silicone covers (to alleviate the coldness and hardness of the straw against my teeth) and a box of paper straws in case I forget my stainless steel ones after washing. The stainless steel straws I purchased come in varying diameters, varying lengths. Some are straight and some are bent. They have a little cloth bag to keep them in when not in use,

along with a right-sized bottle brush. I just have to remember
to decline the straw at the drive-through; maybe one day they
will ask if you need a straw instead of just providing one.

Find the easier or cheaper way to get rid of habits you want
to change. Try to get to the root cause of the problem with five
whys or treat yourself for doing something hard. Experiment
to see what works for you.

FIND YOUR RHYTHM

What habits do you inhabit that are making it hard for you to
eliminate single-use plastics? Identify the intervention-action
gap, evaluate which gap-closing activity might work, and figure
out a way to inhabit this habit to make it better for you and for
the environment.

To replace that unsustainable old habit with a new sustainable habit:

- Make it easier.
- Make it cheaper.
- Ask five whys.
- Bundle it with a reward.

∞

You inhabit your habits—so make them good ones.

When you inhabit your habits and mind the gap—the inter-vention-action gap—you can make space for a world of easier and better choices.

WEEK 9: MAKE SPACE

"Everything you need you already have. You are complete right now, you are a whole, total person, not an apprentice person on the way to someplace else."

– Wayne Dyer

The reason why we haven't created space within our lives for a better self and a better environment typically comes down to three reasons: we don't know any better, we don't have the time, or we don't see the impact.

But if we did know, if we did have time, if we did see the impact, we would create that space. And when we do create space, great things happen. To get to that point a big bang is required. Just like the Big Bang theory of the origination of the universe that says it all started with a "small singularity" that rapidly expanded and continues to expand even in this moment.[55]

According to Merriam-Webster, one of the definitions of singularity is "a point at which the derivative of a given function of a complex variable *does not exist* but every neighborhood of which contains points for which the derivative *does exist*."

Let's walk through this together. From this definition, remove the scary words like *derivative* and *function of a complex variable* and substitute *space* and *need*, and then define *neighborhood* as *everything around us*. Then for each of us:

Singularity is a point at which the space does not exist but everything around us that is needed to create that space does exist.[56]

I am at singularity. You are at singularity. Everyone is at singularity for something. We have everything we need around us to take us from singularity to having the space to do what we need for ourselves, our families, our communities, our world. We just need a big bang that gets us to the point where we look at what is around us and figure out how to create the knowledge, create the time, and realize the impact so that we can begin to expand into that gap, into that space, and allow great things to happen.

We make space not only for ourselves but for others. We make space for others who have skills we don't have. We surround ourselves with superstars, and then let them do their superstar thing. We make space for the quiet ones, who often have quite well-thought-out ideas but are just not willing to fight to be heard. We make space for surprises. We make space for the gift of feedback. We tolerate, even embrace, challenges to our thinking.

Often, that big bang happens when we are on our last straw, just like it did for me when I left corporate America and became a sole proprietor of my own consulting company:

- When we are the most unhappy.
- When things aren't turning out how we thought they would.
- When it looks like we are living the dream, but we are lost in our own personal nightmare.
- When it is all too much.
- When something bad happens in our lives.
- When we know things need to change.

It is all there—everything you need, right now—for you to make the space for what you want to happen.

So what does it look like when someone goes from singularity to space in the rapid expansion of a big bang?

MY BIG BANG JOURNEY

For me, the most recent big bang moment occurred well into the year I decided to hire a personal coach to help with improving me and, along with it, my business. At the beginning of 2019, I was still in a fog from insufficient sleep and feeling tired and complacent. I had been in the doldrums before and knew things needed to change. I was not ready to be done in life. I hired a coach to see if I could get to a better place. I had no idea that the outcome would be a book! Spending a few hours together at the end of October, my coach initiated a discussion to identify what mattered most to me. He managed to turn my incoherent stream-of-consciousness ramblings about plastic bags and straws and nature and leaving a better place for our children into the title for a book, *The Last Straw*, which he informed me I would be writing!

This was definitely a big bang kind of day—a rapid expansion from singularity (everything I needed was already there) to space—enough to fill a book. I rode my coach's confidence until I had my own, well into the book-making process.

MUCH BIGGER BIG BANG JOURNEYS

There are plenty of big bang journeys out there—stories of those "aha" moments when something happens that crystallizes an idea and compels a person to action.

Here I share four big bang stories, one for each type of being in the style of Kolbe from Week 3: Quick Start, Fact Finder, Follow Thru, and Implementor. Of course, I don't really know the Kolbe type of each person mentioned in the following stories; I'm making a guess. The intent is to show that we don't all show up in the same way. My big bang resulted in a book,

and yours might be activism, teaching, building a carbon seques-
tration device, studying the effects of microplastics in the body,
or some other wonderful thing. In each of these cases there is a
story behind the story; we all have a story. The defining factor
is what we decide to do with it.

Quick Start: Greta Thunberg

For Greta Thunberg, the big bang moment came at the tender
age of eight when she learned about climate change. Unable
to reconcile the gravity of the problem with the lack of action,
at the age of eleven she fell into a deep depression, stopped
eating, stopped talking, and lost twenty-two pounds in two
months. She was diagnosed with Asperger syndrome, obses-
sive-compulsive disorder, and selective mutism—she speaks
only when necessary.[57]

In Greta's words: "The first time I heard about global warming,
I thought: that can't be right, no way there is something serious
enough to threaten our very existence. Because otherwise, we
would not be talking about anything else . . . as if a war was
raging."[58] At fifteen, she decided to go on a school strike, posting
herself outside the Swedish Parliament, hoping to get politicians
to act on climate change.[59]

She didn't need to do a lot of research, didn't need to create
systems or organize rallies, didn't need to create a carbon
removal machine; she saw the problem and she acted. Despite

being a child, despite (or because of) being wired differently, despite being alone, she did what she was able to do. A movement rose up because of the stand she took, and in December 2019, at the age of sixteen, Greta Thunberg made the cover of *TIME* magazine as Person of the Year.

Fact Finder: Al Gore

In 2007, former Vice President Al Gore was awarded the Nobel Peace Prize, along with the Intergovernmental Panel on Climate Change for his work on climate change, including the documentary *An Inconvenient Truth*. This movie was preceded by Gore's book *Earth in the Balance: Ecology and Human Spirit*. The big bang moment that inspired the book and his decision not to run for president in 1992, was in 1989 when his six-year-old son was seriously injured after being hit by a car. It was "a trauma so shattering . . . a moment of personal rebirth."[60]

Gore had always been a Fact Finder around environmental issues, but his son's accident refocused him in a way that mobilized him to take action to communicate those facts in a digestible way to the world, through his books and documentaries.

Follow Thru: The Employees of the US Environmental Protection Agency

Over a twenty-five-year period concluding in 1996, the EPA

removed lead, an octane-boosting component, from gasoline. Almost twenty-five years later, we take unleaded gasoline for granted. At the time, it was one of the greatest environmental achievements our nation had experienced. The EPA administrator at that time, Carol Browner, issued a press release noting, "Thousands of tons of lead have been removed from the air, and blood levels of lead in our children are down 70 percent. This means that millions of children will be spared the painful consequences of lead poisoning, such as permanent nerve damage, anemia, or mental retardation."

For the EPA in the early 1970s, the big bang moment came when studies demonstrated that children were overexposed to lead through a variety of sources, including lead from gasoline—found in the air, dust, and soil of urban areas. We can be grateful to the agency bureaucrats that methodically took the regulatory actions necessary to make leaded gasoline, and its effects on children, a thing of the past. These policy makers and scientists continue to work through the environmental problems of our day, with little mention or appreciation. If you are curious about some of these successes, and there are many, visit the EPA's milestones page at www.epa.gov/history.

Implementor: Boyan Slat

With a goal of cleaning up 90 percent of the plastic in the ocean, Boyan Slat and his team are building the technology and equipment to remove plastic from the biggest ocean garbage patch where plastic waste circulates in the Pacific Ocean. This Great Pacific Garbage Patch covers 1.6 million square kilometers—three times the area of France.[61]

For Slat, who is from the Netherlands, his big bang moment came about while scuba diving in Greece as a teenager and seeing more plastic than fish. After graduating from high school he presented his idea for a passive garbage collection system, working with the ocean currents, at a TEDx conference. Months later, with crowdsource funding, he was able to create the Ocean Cleanup project (theoceancleanup.com). He and his team continue to work through the design process, trying out prototypes and learning from each iteration. They have also launched the *Interceptor*, a vessel for the removal of plastic from rivers.

Boyan Slat had an idea and decided to deviate from his college engineering studies to make it happen because he was driven to help clean up the oceans. He did what Implementors do; he built something.

The Ripple Effect of the Big Bang

Finally in the twenty-first century, scientists were able to measure what Einstein had predicted: a ripple effect in the space-time continuum from the origination of the universe in the first moments after the Big Bang.[62] Imagine a stone tossed into a body of water, the waves radiating outward, getting smaller and smaller until they disappear. The ripple effect from the origin of the universe is more like a spiral or a swirl, and unlike the waves radiating outward in water, the effects of the Big Bang will be measurable forever.

That's why the Big Bang is such a powerful metaphor for creating space. We may not always see the effects of what we do, but they are still there, and they will outlast us.

> ## Make space to do the small things, and space will appear to do the big things.

FIGURE OUT WHAT WORKS FOR YOU

You have what you need; it's all there. Something has been niggling at the back of your mind. Name it, face it, and decide what to do with it. You might act now, or you might save it for later. And if you're already doing it, congratulations, you're one of the lucky ones.

FIND YOUR RHYTHM

Are you ready for a big bang moment? Think about what that might be for you personally and for the environment.

> For You

What is your last straw right now, the thing standing on your last nerve? What needs to happen to liberate you, to take you from singularity to space?

All the pieces are already there. Write them down. Find the gaps. Figure out what it takes to fill those holes. Make a plan with dates and milestones. It may not happen overnight but it can happen.

Time passes just the same, whether you work toward your dreams or not.

> For the Environment

What is your last straw when it comes to the world we live in? Climate change-induced flooding or other severe weather events? A litter-infested neighborhood that is negatively impacting your children? Herbicides or pesticides affecting your family, pets, livestock, or wildlife? What needs to happen for you to make space to work on resolving that issue? Follow the model above, and map out a plan!

Let your journey through this book take you from singularity to space—space for a good life and the good of the environment.

Make space . . . so we can share! When we go from singularity

to space, we need to find others who care about the same things
we do, and together, work toward change.

WEEK 10: SHARE

"In vain have you acquired knowledge if you have
not imparted it to others."

– Deuteronomy Rabbah

Information is power—but only when you give it away.
Before you can do that, you must believe that there is enough
of whatever it is to be shared. Then you can decide how you
want to show up in the world: what you want to share and how.

Information is power—
but only when you give it away.

BELIEVE IN ABUNDANCE

Returning to Stephen R. Covey in *The 7 Habits of Highly
Effective People*, he says: "Most people are deeply scripted in
what I call the scarcity mentality. They see life as having only
so much, as though there were only one pie out there. And

if someone were to get a big piece of the pie, it would mean less for everybody else."[63] He goes on to say, "People with a scarcity mentality have a very difficult time sharing recognition and credit, power or profit – even with those who help in the production. They also have a very hard time being genuinely happy for the success of other people. The abundance mentality, on the other hand, flows out of a deep inner sense of personal worth and security. It is the paradigm that there is plenty out there and enough to spare for everybody."[64]

Living in a world where there is enough for everyone just feels plain good. If you're not there, try it. Practice it. When you find yourself responding in a way that belies a scarcity mentality: Stop. Reflect. Reject. Find a different way of thinking. There is indeed enough.

WHAT TO SHARE

Next, figure out what you want to share: What is the burning thing on your mind? Answer the questions: Why is this important? What is my endgame? If it's worth it, you will be willing to step outside your comfort zone. As Sheryl Sandberg asks in *Lean In*, "What would you do if you weren't afraid?"[65] Write a book, maybe? Become an activist? Speak up? Vote? Run for office? Design a device that removes nanoparticles of plastic from the water column? Find your community and take responsibility.[66]

HOW TO SHARE

Figure out your best way to share based on how you like to be: speaking at engagements or on videos; writing books, blogs, social media posts; educating little kids, big kids, adults; serving; joining; becoming involved. You have something someone else needs to hear—share it, with your words, with your deeds, with your kindness. It should almost fall out of you, or at least compel you, to do or be the vehicle for the thing you want to share. The first draft of this book was written in about forty hours over the course of eight weeks, in the midst of Thanksgiving, Christmas, New Year's, and two graduation celebrations. (Editing took about twice as long.)

To write a book, you don't actually have to write a word—you can dictate it and then have it transcribed. You can make a video from your smartphone. You can become a blogger in a day. We live in a time when all things are possible with technology.

When you share, be mindful not to preach (hope that wasn't too preachy). No shaming, no scolding, no embarrassing. Be kind and offer no judgment. Model the behavior you wish to see and admit your own fallibility. People who feel judged will be unable to hear you and you will likely lose the possibility of influencing their behavior. If the situation allows, listen more than you speak and avoid solving a problem no one has asked for help on. Although I will add it's likely counterproductive to listen to someone unwilling to listen to you. We should all challenge ourselves to look at things differently, through another's eyes.

Share Through Education

When my daughter was in fourth grade, there was real tension between her and a classmate. Kaitlin was the child who found the toads, crickets, and any other little critter that might make its way onto the playground, and safeguarded them or built holes in the dirt or nests in the trees for them. As many kids that age do, one little boy crushed everything that moved and took great joy in it. It was clear that Kaitlin was feeling a deep enmity for this classmate and, moved by her genuine pain and her empathy for these tiny creatures, I was concerned the disagreement would escalate. So I created a slide presentation with colorful photos of various grubs and larvae, and what they would become if allowed to survive. I received permission from the teacher to share it with the class. The message was one of education: so if you crush this grub, you won't get this beetle; if you crush this caterpillar, you won't ever get to see this pretty butterfly or moth; and so on. Afterward, Kaitlin reported that the little boy in question had found a cricket missing a leg and brought it to her during recess. I'm sure she found a safe place for it to finish out its little life. It's not as though she and the little boy became fast friends, but at least they never came to blows.

Sometimes education isn't a classroom presentation;

sometimes it is through modeling the behavior you hope to see in others. Behavior can be a more powerful influencer than words.

Share Through Modeling Behavior

Trained as a biologist, I generally thought about ecology in terms of preserving a population (e.g., habitat preservation) rather than efforts to preserve an individual animal. Then I had a daughter who only saw the individual. Seeing insects and spiders as little life forces, as she did, transformed my way of thinking. Now, I will move insects and spiders outside, rather than killing them, if at all possible. And I have made a deal with the wasps: if they will stay out of my way (including off my house), I won't bother them. For the ones who think our home is a good place to build a nest, I have an eco-friendly spray that gets rid of them and their nest so they won't come back. But it doesn't destroy the balance in the microhabitat that supports the lizards, moths, butterflies, orb weavers, and beetles that hang out there. Because of that balance, we have few problems with bugs coming into the house; although my daughter did show me a spider friend hiding in the threshold of an outside door near her room. She's not worried about him, as she knows he's only interested in smaller insects and won't bother her.

Share for Others, If Not Yourself

Learn what works. If you won't do it for yourself, think about the people (or animals) you care about. My daughter Kaitlin hates getting any kind of shot. When she was small, it took both a nurse and me to hold her tiny little person down to ensure she got her immunizations. She still will do anything to put off getting a shot. But with the knowledge that some of the kids she instructed at the horse-riding center were immune-compromised, and seriously so, she got her shot knowing that she could not forgive herself if she didn't do everything possible to reduce the likelihood of transmitting the flu to her precious riders.

Kaitlin handled a baby raccoon that was temporarily trapped in a fallen tree (the momma raccoon was waiting for nightfall to move the baby). Weeks later, that raccoon could be found at the cat's food bowl accepting literal handouts from Kaitlin. After imploring her to stop, I finally explained the harsh realities. If she was nipped, even accidentally, we would not only have to take her in for rabies vaccinations, but we would also have to hunt down the raccoon so that it could be tested for rabies. And the only way to do that is to access the brain stem—in other words, the raccoon would have to be killed (even though a case has not been reported in our county in forty years).

She wouldn't take action (flu shot) or stop taking action (feeding a raccoon) for herself, but she would do it to protect others.

Share by Positive Peer Pressure

Sometimes positive peer pressure works. Visiting friends in the Puget Sound area, we could see how clean and litter free the area was. Our friends said no one would ever not pick up after their dog, as it would be too embarrassing to be called out on it. And of course, walking along the beach with them, we found a pile. We collected it out of a desire to keep these clear waters in their pristine condition, knowing that dog feces are a major contributor to stormwater pollution. Many do not realize the hazard to our water quality that pet poop presents. The eighty-four million dogs living in the US create 22.9 trillion pounds of waste per year.[67] During rain events, dog waste and the pathogens (bacteria, parasites, and viruses) and pollutants (nitrogen and phosphorus) it carries reach our creeks and rivers by way of storm drains and sheet flow.[68]

Another easy way to contribute to your community is to report illegal dumping. Once dumping starts, it seems to give others license to dump. Our county has a phone app anyone can use to report illegal dumping. The county will investigate to see if they can find out who is responsible and also pick up and recycle or dispose of the waste. Clean places tend to remain clean, and dumping grounds only get worse.

Sharing matters. Do it your way, in your time, through your medium, but understand that if you don't share, there are real consequences.

UNDERSTAND THE COSTS OF NOT SHARING

Imagine a world where *Silent Spring* had not been written. Rachel Carson published this seminal book in the same year I was born and she died at around my current age. Such a short life, yet so much accomplished.[69] In the acknowledgments, she writes of her inspiration for the book, her friend's report that her songbirds were dying—falling out of the sky it seemed almost—due to the aggressive use of pesticides.[70] She was at a moment of singularity and was compelled to make the space to do something about it—her big bang moment.

Rachel Carson was a nature writer who worked for the US Fish and Wildlife Services during the 1930s and 1940s. She wrote several books in the 1940s and 1950s, and in 1962 published *Silent Spring*, the book that some say launched the environmental movement. Her revelations awoke the public to the devastation wrought upon ecosystems throughout the country, as DDT, chlordane, heptachlor, and other pesticides, all banned now, were applied as a panacea against the pests impacting the agriculture and timber industries.

Her depressing account of case after case of birds, fish, and other animals being killed off or otherwise affected, in some cases for generations, by the over-application of pesticides is a window into a time when a lack of forethought, greed, and blind ignorance led us down a destructive path, the effects of which are still evident today. Pesticide residuals that are still detected to varying degrees in fatty tissue, breast milk, and food sources give us a glimpse of how bad it might have been were it not for the environmental revolution that *Silent Spring* launched.

The lesser-known part of the story is that even as Carson was writing the book and defending her position to those in government and industry, she was fighting an aggressive form of breast cancer. The fight for her life, which she lost eighteen months after the book was published, provided a singular focus for her work and insulated her from the well-orchestrated character assassination by the chemical industry.

Six years after Carson's death, the first Earth Day was commemorated and Congress passed the National Environmental Policy Act, which established the Environmental Protection Agency. Even though considerable progress has been made since the book was published, it is an important reminder that "we, like all other living creatures, are part of the vast ecosystems of the earth, part of the whole stream of life."[71]

There is a very real cost to not sharing our story, knowledge, wisdom, power, kindness, compassion. We are experiencing that cost right now in the form of more severe weather events and a painfully forced adaptation to climate change because the leaders in developed nations failed to act.

Just as when we toss that stone into the water and tiny waves radiate outward, we can't help but affect others. A big splash isn't required. Acting in a way aligned to our natural way of being is all it takes and we might just have a bigger impact than we ever thought possible.

Remember the ripple effect from the Big Bang? There's a ripple effect when we share, even in small ways.

Our impact, no matter what it is, will outlast us. That is our legacy.

There is a very real cost to not sharing.

FIGURE OUT WHAT WORKS FOR YOU

Today, sharing ideas, information, and inspiration is much easier. Websites like www.trashisfortossers.com, for example, are just a search away. We can find podcasts on just about anything— including sustainability. If we can consume it, we can create it. We live in a country where anyone can do almost anything.

The only thing separating you from any other influencer out there is confidence. Have the confidence to create your content, in your medium, in your chosen forum. And if you don't have the confidence right now, then ride someone else's confidence in you; that's what I did in writing this book.

FIND YOUR RHYTHM

Ralph Waldo Emerson said, "Your actions speak so loudly, I cannot hear what you are saying." How can you make your actions congruent with your words (and thoughts)?

> For You

How do you demonstrate an abundance mentality? What do you keep coming back to that you want to influence? Why?

What is holding you back? Remember, there are costs to not sharing. What are the costs to others, and to you, if you don't share?

What is your medium? Say it, show it, write it, build it.

> For the Environment

How can that abundance mentality be leveraged for good, in your family, your work, your community, your world? Revisit the swaps and shifts at the end of this chapter, and turn it into a checklist, adding your own items.

No big thing happens overnight. There are many small steps in between. You will not become a zero-waste household in one day (if that is your aim), but you can start by separating out recyclables. Tackling the small stuff helps us get the skills and confidence to tackle the big stuff. And you get to decide what the big stuff is. I tested this notion of small things making for big changes on my son. The conversation went like this: "If you don't believe small acts can make a difference, stop brushing your teeth." He said, "But brushing your teeth is important!" Exactly. When we value the big results, in this case a beautiful, cavity-free smile, we find value in the small steps that get us there, like brushing our teeth for a few minutes each day.

When you share your abundance (whatever that might be) you make people and you make the planet a better place. So share. Share your time, your money, all in a manner consistent with your natural state of being.

A WORK IN PROGRESS

"Once we start to act, hope is everywhere."

– Greta Thunberg

This is not the end, it's the beginning. Once we are mindful of what we are doing and the choices we are making, we will become aware of more opportunities to influence people to be better and help make the planet a better place. Small changes beget big changes.

You know best what comes into your home, where the opportunities are, and what challenges you face. There are far more opportunities than I can write in a book or can even imagine.

And above all, give yourself a break. You are trying. You cannot do it all alone.

The societal systems put in place long before we were born are in silent running mode.[72] We don't even see them. Just 100 companies are responsible for more than 70 percent of greenhouse gas emissions since 1988.[73] We inherited an economy based on energy and plastics from fossil fuels, so we have to live in that world while we work to change it—all while juggling family, work, health, and everything else.

Maybe being mindful of the small things will get us to the big things, like investing our time in research on the companies we as consumers want to support.

We have to live in the current system even as we work to change it.

Hopefully you are sleeping better, playing more, being yourself, spending your money and time intentionally, serving others, shedding negativity, stretching yourself, inhabiting good habits, making space for good things to happen, and sharing your wisdom with the rest of us!

Even with all of that, you may not have achieved the results for which you had hoped. Then you would be just like me: a work in progress. The first time I remembered to use my own metal fork in place of the plastic forks they give out at the restaurants I frequent, I thought I threw the fork out with the paper plate. Turns out, it fell out of the cloth bag into my car. Sigh.

I like to think of what Samuel Beckett wrote in *Worstward Ho*, "Ever tried. Ever failed. No matter. Try again. Fail again. Fail better."

Every failure becomes an opportunity to do better, and better people means a better planet.

#betterpeoplebetterplanet

A BRIEF NOTE ON SCIENCE

"Scientists do change their minds in the face of new
evidence, but this is a strength of science, not a weakness."

– Naomi Oreskes

There is a lot of seemingly conflicting information out there
that can make us want to throw up our hands and say, "I give
up!" This is especially true when we are trying so hard to make
positive changes and create new habits—small things like, do
we go with cloth or paper or plastic bags, and big things, like
what should our community be doing to adapt to a changing
climate? Not only do we need to find what works for us, we
want to base it on good science. How can we make sure our
choices are grounded in scientific fact?

We make decisions based on our beliefs and values. In the
context used here, a belief is an acceptance that a statement is

true or that something exists; a value is a person's principles or standards of behavior. Science, the body of knowledge on a particular subject, helps shape our beliefs but is not always easily available to us, so we have to make an effort to *find* the science.[74] There is a methodology you can follow to help you find the science on just about anything:

1.   Get the facts. Expose yourself to science-based information sources.
2.   Be curious. Learn as much as you can.
3.   Be skeptical. Be mindful of accepting anecdotes as fact.
4.   Look for confirmation. Get second opinions from other scientists.
5.   Accept that we make value judgments. Not every aspect of our decision-making is based in fact, nor does it need to be.
6.   Be willing to be influenced if new facts arise.

Sometimes we wonder if we can trust the science we find. Harvard Professor Naomi Oreskes, author of "Why Trust Science," an essay in the November 18, 2019, issue of *TIME* magazine, helps us understand how we get good science:

"A key aspect of scientific judgment is that it is done collectively . . . in modern science, no claim gets accepted until it has been vetted by dozens, if not hundreds, of heads. In areas that have been contested, like climate science and vaccine safety, it's thousands. This is why we are generally justified in not worrying too much if a single scientist, even a very famous one, dissents from the consensus. The odds that the lone dissenter is right, and everyone else is wrong, are probably in most cases close to zero. This is why diversity in science—the more people looking at a claim from different angles—is important."

Peer-reviewed scientific journal articles are among the best ways of getting science, and this kind of information is more available to us than ever before. Google Scholar (scholar.google. com) is a source accessible to everyone with Internet access. But for every paper you read, you must consider:

- Who wrote it? What are their affiliations? Are they an independent researcher?
- Who paid for it? Follow the money. How did this influence the study?
- What is the scope of the study? What is excluded from the scope? What assumptions were made?
- How will the paper be used? Is it being used as intended?
- Was it peer reviewed? Who were the reviewers?

For example, there are studies suggesting that based on a life-cycle assessment, plastic bags are the way to go. However, these studies are typically supported, directly or indirectly, by the plastics industry, they tend to compare plastic bags to paper bags (instead of reusable bags), and do not consider the health impacts on us (microplastics have now been found in humans);[75] the fish we eat (a source of the microplastics in humans);[76] our wildlife, in particular, marine life and marine mammals; the clogging of waterways; the visual blight of littered bags on our communities (and the toll of the associated stress on our bodies); and the limits of our precious landfill space, among other things.

An oft-cited statistic is that it takes 131 uses of a cotton bag to beat a single use of a plastic bag (based on energy and water resource usage, not considering the impacts listed above). Since we have had our cloth bags for more than ten years and use about five bags a week to carry groceries, we have replaced 2,600 plastic bags during this time! And our reusable cloth bags are still going strong. Reusable bags are the better alternative when *all* potential environmental impacts are considered.[77] Just be sure and wash them regularly and avoid using them for raw meat trays; try a washable plastic cooler instead. And if you have a legitimate need for a plastic bag, use it without apology and then be sure it is properly recycled (most national retailers will take any retail plastic bag for recycling). If you reuse it and it can't be recycled, then dispose of it in the trash. There is no plastic bag police.

When we apply the science and share it with others, we can do so thoughtfully using a model established by Rotarians years ago.[78] Their four-way test goes like this:

1. Is it the *truth*?
2. Is it *fair* to all concerned?
3. Will it build *goodwill* and better friendships?
4. Will it be *beneficial* to all concerned?[79]

You've got this. Trust the science and share it well.

Find the science.

FIND YOUR RHYTHM

Practice finding the science on things that matter to you. Get curious and be scrupulous about your sources of information.

> For You

Find the science on the habit you are having the most problems with, such as sleep, play, being, spending, shedding, stretching, habits, and let the science help form the basis for your next step forward.

> For the Environment

Find the science on something you have wondered about in the area of environmental protection or sustainability and let the science help form the basis to take action.

It may take a little bit of work and a lot of separating out junk science, but we are better equipped than ever to find the science.

SHIFTS AND SWAPS

INSTEAD OF . . .	DO THIS . . .
WHEN SHOPPING, INSTEAD OF	
Using single-use plastic bags,	use reusable grocery bags.
Using single-use plastic produce bags,	leave the items loose or use reusable produce bags.
Purchasing over-packaged products,	choose products with less packaging.
Throwing plastic bags in the trash or recycling,	return plastic bags to retailers on your next trip.
IN THE KITCHEN, INSTEAD OF	
Having meat with every meal,	eat a diet high in whole grains and vegetables; experiment with meatless Mondays, tofu Tuesdays, and seitan Sundays (seitan is made out of gluten).
Eating meat from animals raised in industrial feedlots,	choose meat, dairy, and eggs from pasture-raised farms.
Buying milk in plastic jugs or waxed cardboard cartons,	buy milk and juice in returnable glass jugs, or non-returnable glass or metal containers.
Throwing away excess or spoiled food,	plan meals and make purchases to reduce food waste.

IN THE KITCHEN, INSTEAD OF (CONTINUED)

Disposing of fruit and uncooked vegetable waste in the trash,	compost fruit and vegetable waste, along with eggshells and coffee grounds.
Using plastic wrap,	invest in glass containers with reusable lids for leftover food.
Using paper napkins and towels,	use cloth napkins and towels and wash with the next load of clothes
Running partial loads in the dishwasher,	fill the dishwasher before running.
Drinking coffee or tea from single use K-Cups,	use a percolating coffee pot or find a company that takes K-Cup returns.

AROUND THE HOUSE, INSTEAD OF

Letting all your household waste go to the landfill,	choose a trash pickup service that offers curbside recycling, or separate and take recyclables to your county recycler.
Using plastic trash bags,	use compostable trash bags.
Using plastic disposable diapers,	use cloth diapers or a diaper service.
Celebrating with balloons,	decorate with flowers (and then compost them).
Lighting with fluorescent light bulbs,	replace bulbs with LED bulbs when they go out.
Leaving phones on chargers and other small appliances plugged in,	unplug chargers and small appliances when not in use.

AROUND THE HOUSE, INSTEAD OF (CONTINUED)	
Leaving computers, monitors, and speakers on all the time,	turn them off when not in use.
Running ceiling fans all the time,	turn off the ceiling fan when not in the room.
Leaving the lights on,	turn them off when you leave the room.
Using toxic chemical pesticides inside your home,	use mechanical means to remove insects and spiders from your home.
Buying ice for your cooler,	reuse plastic jugs by filling with water, freezing, and using as ice packs.
Printing materials to read them,	send documents to an e-reader.
Cooling or heating your home to the same temperature year round,	turn down the temperature when it's cold; turn it up when it's warm.
Using electricity to cool or warm your home,	open the windows to allow for natural cooling and heating.
Losing energy through gaps, poor insulation, and energy-inefficient windows,	conduct an energy audit of your home (sometimes electricity providers will do this for free).
Maintaining the water heater at very high temperature,	reduce the temperature on the water heater; insulate the heater.
Getting natural gas or electricity from fossil fuels,	switch to a renewable electricity provider or install solar panels.
Taking electricity from the grid,	look into solar panels or wind energy (depending on where you live).

IN YOUR PERSONAL CARE ROUTINE, INSTEAD OF	
Using wipes to remove makeup,	use washcloths.
Flossing your teeth with polymer floss in plastic dispensers,	use compostable dental lace in a refillable glass container.
Using plastic, single-use flossers,	use dental lace or wooden toothpicks.
Using plastic, disposable razors,	use metal, reusable razors.
Using Kleenex tissue,	use toilet paper and flush it instead of tossing it in the trash.
Flushing used contact lens,	dispose of contact lens in the trash.
Disposing of used cotton balls in the trash,	compost used cotton balls.
Using Q-tips made from plastic,	choose Q-tips made from cardboard.
WHEN DINING OUT, INSTEAD OF	
Using plastic straws,	decline the straw, or use stainless steel or paper straws.
Using Styrofoam takeout containers and single-use plastic containers,	bring your own reusable takeout containers and utensils.
Single-use water bottles and Styrofoam cups,	use a refillable water bottle or reusable mug.

WHEN USING TRANSPORTATION, INSTEAD OF	
Commuting daily with single occupancy,	rideshare, use public transportation, or work remotely when possible.
Driving to your destination,	walk or bike.
Flying to your destination,	have a remote conference or meeting, or drive or take a boat.
Defaulting to one-day or two-day shipping every time with Amazon Prime,	choose five-day shipping if you don't need it right away.
Removing the gas nozzle too quickly and dripping fuel,	pause when the gas is done pumping and avoid drips and fumes.
Changing out vehicles frequently,	keep your vehicle as long as you can, and when it is no longer working, scrap it and buy an electric vehicle (as long as your energy source is renewable).
Printing your boarding pass,	use a digital boarding pass.
Using a plastic hotel key card,	use a digital key card (if using a plastic card, return for reuse, or recycle as a last resort).
Buying bottled water,	carry a refillable water bottle.
Accepting a paper receipt (air travel, hotel, rental car),	request an e-receipt.

IN THE YARD AND GARDEN, INSTEAD OF	
Mowing and watering a lawn,	plant trees, wildflower beds, native plants, rain gardens, and xeriscapes, and skip the fertilizer.
Planting store-bought, non-native flowers,	broadcast regional wildflower seeds.
Fertilizing your lawn or using herbicides,	use grasses that work in your area and allow them to respond to seasonal and weather variations.
Mowing when not really needed,	skip mowing when you can, especially outside the growing season.
Watering the sidewalk and driveway, or watering during the rain,	quit watering entirely, but if you must, maintain your sprinkler system to water only the grass, and only when needed.
Using pesticides,	use mechanical methods (crushing aphids with your fingers, for example), or eco-friendly methods (ladybugs and marigolds, for example), or eco-friendly sprays (to discourage wasps from nesting in your home, for example).
Leaving litter on the ground,	pick it up and sort it for recycling.
Passing by dumped trash,	report illegal dumping.
Throwing cigarette butts on the ground,	collect cigarette butts and recycle when possible; dispose of them in the trash when not possible.
Allowing dog feces to be deposited on walkways, roads, and in the yard, where children can be exposed to it, and where it will wash into waterways,	collect and dispose of dog droppings in the trash.

WHEN EVALUATING FINANCES, INSTEAD OF	
Having a financial investment portfolio adversely impacted by climate change,	invest according to Environmental, Social, and Governance (ESG) factors.

WHEN TALKING WITH OTHERS, INSTEAD OF	
Avoiding the topics of environmental issues, sustainability, and climate change,	talk about it! Become active on issues you care about: blogging; posting on social media; writing elected officials; attending protests; running for office; sharing sustainability struggles and successes with your family, friends, and neighbors.

ACKNOWLEDGMENTS

First, thank *you* for being one of the hopeful ones. I also want to thank Jenny McKinney, my sister, for being my biggest fan from the very beginning and for showing me what it looks like to be a person full of joy and hope; Jonathan Sprinkles, for his encouragement and support in pushing, pulling, and prodding me from singularity to finding space, the title and subtitle for the book, the idea for the Big Bang theory analogy, and the hashtag #betterpeoplebetterplanet; Lorrie Gonzales, for introducing me to Kolbe through her own story; Mark Katchen and George Walker, for introducing me to *Conversational Capacity;* my brilliant cover and interior designer, Vanessa Mendozzi; Grace Kerina, for an editorial assessment (two rounds!) filled with love and practical information; Janina Lawrence for copy editing; Katie Salisbury for thoughtful proofreading; and each friend and family member who was kind enough to take the time to review the manuscript and offer the gift of feedback: my sister, Jenny; my husband, Lars; my kids, Kait and Nic; my cousin, Linda Postal Marshall; and my colleagues, Trisha Gupta and Kathryn Burch Lintner.

ABOUT THE AUTHOR

Joyce Kristiansson has a bachelor's degree in biological sciences and a master's degree in environmental management. She has a consulting practice, Kristiansson LLC, that specializes in helping companies improve their environmental performance through self-sustaining management systems. Joyce lives in Houston, Texas, along with her husband of almost twenty-five years, Lars. They enjoy spending time reveling in the wide variety of nature in their backyard and wherever they find it, and hearing the stories their adult children, Nic and Kait, have to share.

You can reach the author at joyce@thelaststrawbook.com, through the book's website, thelaststrawbook.com, and on the Facebook page, The Last Straw, and the associated group of the same name.

END NOTES

1 United Nations, Department of Economic Social Affairs. "World Population Prospects 2019." *www.population. un.org/wpp/Publications/Files/WPP2019_Highlights.pdf*. Web. 5 Jan 2020.

2 Plastic Oceans. "The Facts." *www.plasticoceans.org/the-facts/*. Web. 5 Jan 2020.

3 Chen, Angus. "Ninety-nine Percent of the Ocean's Plastic Is Missing." *Science Magazine*, 30 Jun 2014, *www. sciencemag.org/news/2014/06/ninety-nine-percent-oceans-plastic-missing*. Web. 5 Jan 2020.

4 Clear, James. "How Long Does It Take to Form a New Habit? (Backed by Science)." *JamesClear.com*. *www. jamesclear.com/new-habit*. Web. 26 Dec 2019.

5 Lally, P., van Jaarsveld, C.H.M., Potts, H.W.W. and Wardle, J. (2010), How are habits formed: Modelling habit formation in the real world. Eur. J. Soc. Psychol., *www. onlinelibrary.wiley.com/doi/full/10.1002/ejsp.674*.

6 Moving Beyond Cancer. "12 Weeks of Chemotherapy Is Equal to a Decade of Physical Decline in Terms of Cardiorespiratory Fitness." *www.movingbeyondcancer.com. au/latest-research/18-12-weeks-of-chemotherapy-is-equal-to-a-decade-of-physical-decline-in-terms-of-cardiorespi-ratory-fitness*. Web. 22 Dec 2019.

7 CPAP stands for Continuous Positive Airway Pressure.

8 American Sleep Apnea Association. "What does 'AHI'

represent?" 31 Aug 2017. *www.sleephealth.org/ufaqs/what-is-ahi-represent/*. Web. 28 Dec 2019.

9   Harvard Medical School. Division of Sleep Medicine. Apnea. "Understanding the Results." 8 Feb 2018. *www.healthysleep.med.harvard.edu/sleep-apnea/diagnos-ing-osa/understanding-results*. Web. 28 Dec 2019.

10   APAP stands for Automatic Positive Airway Pressure.

11   Martin, Rachel. "Amy Poehler Leads a Girls' Trip with 'Some of the Funniest People in the World,'" NPR. *Morning Edition*. 24 May 2019. *www.npr.org/2019/05/24/726281571/amy-poehler-leads-a-girls-trip-with-some-of-the-funniest-people-in-the-world*.

12   Waxman, Olivia B. "9 Questions." *TIME*. 2-9 Sep 2019: 116. Print.

13   BaHammam, Ahmed S. and Aljohara S. Almeneessier. "Dreams and Nightmares in Patients with Obstructive Sleep Apnea: A Review." *Front. Neurol.* 22 Oct 2019. *www.doi.org/10.3389/fneur.2019.01127*.

14   National Sleep Foundation. "Findings Reveal Brain Mechanisms at Work During Sleep." *www.sleepfoundation.org/articles/findings-reveal-brain-mechanisms-work-during-sleep*. Web. 7 Dec 2019.

15   National Sleep Foundation. "What Happens When You Sleep?" *www.sleepfoundation.org/articles/what-happens-when-you-sleep*. Web. 7 Dec 2019.

16   Kemmis, Sam. "The Science of Sleep and Productivity."
     Zapier.com. 7 Mar 2019. *www.zapier.com/blog/slee-
     p-and-productivity/.* Web. 7 Dec 2019.

17   Carter, Matthew, MD. "The Science of Sleep (and the Art
     of Productivity)." *TEDx North Adams.* 22 Mar 2018. *www.
     youtube.com/watch?v=894jQkeewiU.*

18   Mawer, Rudy. "17 Proven Tips to Sleep Better at Night."
     Healthline. 27 Feb 2020. *www.healthline.com/nutrition/17-
     tips-to-sleep-better.* Web. 26 Dec 2019.

19   Brown, Stuart, MD. "The Science of Play: Enjoying a
     Fulfilling Life by Retaining our Ability and Right to Play."
     Playcore. 28 Nov 2018. *www.playcore.com/news/enjoying-
     a-fulfilling-life-by-retaining-our-ability-and-right-to-play.*
     Web. 21 Dec 2019.

20   Tartakovsky, Margarita. "The Importance of Play for
     Adults." 8 Jul 2018. *www.psychcentral.com/blog/the-im-
     portance-of-play-for-adults/.* Web. 22 Dec 2019.

21   The Aluminum Association. "Recycling." *www.aluminum.
     org/industries/production/recycling.* Web. 22 Dec 2019.

22   Brown, Stuart, MD. "Play is more than
     just fun." *TED.* May 2008. *ted.com/talks/
     stuart_brown_play_is_more_than_just_fun.*

23   American Heart Association. "American Heart Associ-
     ation Recommendations for Physical Activity in Adults
     and Kids." *www.heart.org/en/healthy-living/fitness/*

fitness-basics/aha-recs-for-physical-activity-in-adults. Web. 29 Dec 2019.

24 Kolbe Corp. *www.kolbe.com/.*

25 Vojinovic, Ivana. "Job Satisfaction Statistics: Keep Your Workers Happy and Your Business Healthy." Small Biz Genius. 9 Sep 2019. *www.smallbizgenius.net/by-the-numbers/job-satisfaction-statistics/#gref.* Web. 29 Dec 2019.

26 Thomas, Kenneth W. and Ralph H. Kilmann. "Thomas-Kilmann Conflict Mode Instrument Profile and Interpretive Report." CPP, Inc. 2007.

27 Thomas, Kenneth W. and Gail Fann Thomas. *Introduction to Conflict and Teams: Enhancing Team Performance Using the TKI.* CPP, Inc. 2004.

28 Weber, Craig. *Conversational Capacity: The Secret to Building Successful Teams that Perform When the Pressure Is On.* McGraw-Hill Education. 2013.

29 "'I' Message." *GoodTherapy.com.* 14 Feb 2018. *www.goodtherapy.org/blog/psychpedia/i-message.* Web. 29 Dec 2019.

30 Carlos, Juan. "How Americans Spend Their Money, in One Chart." *HowMuch.* 10 Oct 2019. *www.howmuch.net/articles/breakdown-average-american-spending.* Web. 29 Dec 2019.

31 Fottrell, Quentin. "People Spend Most of Their Waking Hours Staring at Screens." *MarketWatch.* 4 Aug 2018.

www.marketwatch.com/story/people-are-spending-most-of-their-waking-hours-staring-at-screens-2018-08-01. Web. 29 Dec 2019.

32   Chatzky, Jean. "Newsflash: The F***ing Latte Is a F***ing Metaphor." *HerMoney*. 29 Jul 2019. *www.hermoney.com/save/budgeting/the-fing-latte-is-a-fing-metaphor/*. Web. 29 Dec 2019.

33   Curtin, Melanie. "In an 8-Hour Day, the Average Worker Is Productive for This Many Hours." *Inc.*. 21 Jul 2016. *www.inc.com/melanie-curtin/in-an-8-hour-day-the-average-worker-is-productive-for-this-many-hours.html*. Web. 1 Mar 2020.

34   Covey, Stephen R. *The 7 Habits of Highly Effective People*. Simon & Schuster. 1990.

35   Segal, Jeanne, PhD, and Lawrence Robinson. "Volunteering and Its Surprising Benefits." *HelpGuide*. June 2019. *www.helpguide.org/articles/healthy-living/volunteering-and-its-surprising-benefits.htm*. Web. 26 Dec 2019.

36   Segal, et al., 2019.

37   Neid, Jennifer. "The 'Helper's High' Is Why Volunteering Makes You Feel So Good." *Simplemost*. 26 Sep 2018. *www.simplemost.com/the-helpers-high-is-why-volunteering-makes-you-feel-so-good/*. Web. 26 Dec 2019.

38   "Church Trends and Statistics." *Church Executive* magazine. 2 Feb 2019. *www.churchexecutive.com/archives/*

church-trends-statistics. Web. 26 Dec 2019.

39   Walsh, Nuala. "Living on 'Planet You': Why Nobody Notices
      Your Flaws Half as Much as You Think." 9 Aug 2018.
      www.*thriveglobal.com/stories/living-on-planet-you-why-*
      nobody-notices-your-flaws-half-as-much-as-you-think/.
      Web. 5 Jan 2020.

40   Parker, Laura. "Here's How Much Plastic Trash Is Lit-
      tering the Earth." *National Geographic*. 30 Dec 2018.
      www.nationalgeographic.com/news/2017/07/plastic-pro-
      duced-recycling-waste-ocean-trash-debris-environment/.
      Web. 22 Mar 2020.

41   Shapley, Haley. "Why Plastic Bags Can't Go with the
      Regular Recycling." *Earth911*. 20 Mar 2019. *www.*
      earth911.com/business-policy/video-plastic-bag-recy-
      cling/. Web. 12 Jan 2020.

42   Weber, 2013.

43   Gibbens, Sarah. "A Brief History of How Plastic Straws
      Took Over the World." *National Geographic*. 2 Jan 2019.
      www.nationalgeographic.com/environment/2018/07/news-
      plastic-drinking-straw-history-ban/. Web. 7 Dec 2019.

44   "US Breast Cancer Statistics." *BreastCancer.org*. 27 Jan
      2020. *www.breastcancer.org/symptoms/understand_bc/*
      statistics. Web. 7 Dec 2019.

45   This book was written in the fall of 2019 and edited in the
      spring of 2020. COVID-19 has made 2020 very interesting,

and not in a good way.

46 Amabile, Teresa and Steven J. Kramer. "The Power of Small Wins." *Harvard Business Review*. May 2011. *www.hbr.org/2011/05/the-power-of-small-wins*.

47 Chang, Ailsa. "Why People with Climate Change Concerns Don't Always Do What's Best for the Environment." NPR. *All Things Considered*. 13 Dec 2019. *www.npr.org/2019/12/13/787952258/why-people-with-climate-change-concerns-dont-always-do-what-s-best-for-the-envir*.

48 Miller, Ryan W.. "Oral-B Glide Floss Tied to Potentially Toxic PFAS Chemicals. Study Suggests." *USA Today*. 10 Jan 2019. *www.usatoday.com/story/news/nation/2019/01/09/oral-b-glide-floss-toxic-pfas-chemicals-study/2530661002/*. Web. 30 Dec 2019.

49 Breau, Jodi. "Our Story." Dental Lace, Inc., Web. 30 Dec 2019. *www.dentallace.com/pages/about-us*.

50 Chang, 2019.

51 Chang, 2019.

52 Van Vliet, Vincent. "Sakichi Toyoda." *Toolshero*. 2014. *www.toolshero.com/toolsheroes/sakichi-toyoda/*. Web. 31 Dec 2019.

53 Brewer, Judson. "How to Break Up with Your Bad Habits." *Harvard Business Review*. 5 Dec 2019, *www.hbr.org/2019/12/how-to-break-up-with-your-bad-habits*.

54   Wharton School of Business. "Using 'The Hunger Games' to Encourage Healthier Choices." *Knowledge@Wharton*. 19 Nov 2013. *www.knowledge.wharton.upenn.edu/article/researchers-used-hunger-games-encourage-healthier-choices/*. Web. 1 Jan 2020.

55   Howell, Elizabeth. "What Is the Big Bang Theory." *Space.com*. 7 Nov 2017. *www.space.com/25126-big-bang-theory.html*. Web. 16 Nov 2019.

56   In fact, I'll never know if I was bad at math or just an over-tired college student; I had to take calculus in college but made the mistake of taking an 8:00 a.m. class in a summer course while working full time. I believe I made it to class most of the time but also slept through it resulting in a passing grade with only a passing memory to match—so humor me on this analogy.

57   Thunberg, Greta. "School Strike for Climate – Save the World by Changing the Rules." *TEDx Stockholm*. 12 Dec 2018. *www.youtube.com/watch?v=EAmmUIEsN9A&t=1m46s*.

58   We Don't Have Time. "Greta Thunberg: 'Sweden Is Not a Role Model,'" *Medium*. 24 Aug 2018. *www.medium.com/@wedonthavetime/greta-thunberg-sweden-is-not-a-role-model-6ce96d6b5f8b*. Web. 1 Mar 2020.

59   Crouch, David. "The Swedish 15-year-old Who's Cutting Class to Fight the Climate Crisis." *The Guardian*. 1 Sep 2018. *www.theguardian.com/science/2018/sep/01/*

swedish-15-year-old-cutting-class-to-fight-the-climate-crisis. Web. 1 Mar 2020.

60   Tumulty, Karen. "Democratic Convention: The Women Who Made Al Gore." *TIME*. 21 Aug 2000. *www.content.time.com/time/magazine/article/0,9171,997752-2,00.html*. Web. 1 Mar 2020.

61   The Ocean Cleanup. "The Great Pacific Garbage Patch Explained." *www.theoceancleanup.com/great-pacific-garbage-patch/?gclid=Cj0KCQjwjoH0BRD6ARIsAEWO9DtHaqeVG-8kAdescRAhPRZybsLlZdvcqP-1ZLq-maQ8E_90uLF5qwKAaAm6jEALw_wcB*. Web. 29 Mar 2020.

62   Grossman, Lisa. "First Glimpse of Big Bang Ripples from Universe's Birth." *New Scientist*. 17 Mar 2014. *www.newscientist.com/article/dn25235-first-glimpse-of-big-bang-ripples-from-universes-birth/*. Web. 6 Mar 2020.

63   Covey, 1990.

64   Covey, 1990.

65   Sandberg, Sheryl. *Lean In: Women, Work, and the Will to Lead*. New York: Alfred A. Knopf. 2013.

66   Neubauer, Luisa. "Why You Should Become a Climate Activist." *TEDx Youth@München*. Jul 2019. *www.ted.com/talks/luisa_neubauer_why_you_should_be_a_climate_activist*.

67   Alliance for the Chesapeake Bay. "Scoop the Poop."

Reduce Your Stormwater. 2 Oct 2015. *www.stormwater.allianceforthebay.org/runoff-busters/scoop-the-poop*. Web. 4 Jan 2020.

68   Keep It Clean Partnership. "Keep Our Creeks Clean. Clean Up After Your Dog!" *www.keepitcleanpartnership.org/pollution-prevention/scoop-the-poop/*. Web. 4 Jan 2020.

69   Kristiansson, Joyce. *"The 50ᵗʰ Anniversary of Silent Spring."* EAST Newsletter. Dec 2012.

70   Carson, Rachel. *Silent Spring*. Houghton Mifflin. 1962.

71   Lear, Linda. Introduction to *Silent Spring*. Houghton Mifflin Harcourt. 2002.

72   Gardiner, Beth. "Why You Shouldn't Feel Too Guilty About Flying." *CNN Travel*. 13 Jan 2020. *www.cnn.com/travel/article/flying-guilt/index.html*. Web. 21 Jan 2020.

73   Riley, Tess. "Just 100 Companies Responsible for 71% of Global Emissions, Study Says." *The Guardian*. 10 Jul 2017. *www.theguardian.com/sustainable-business/2017/jul/10/100-fossil-fuel-companies-investors-responsible-71-global-emissions-cdp-study-climate-change*. Web. 21 Jan 2020.

74   von Winterfeldt, Detlof. "Bridging the Gap Between Science and Decision Making." *Proceedings of the National Academy of Sciences* 110. supplement 3 (August 20, 2013): 14055-14061. *www.pnas.org/content/110/Supplement_3/14055*.

75 Gibbens, Sarah. "You Eat Thousands of Bits of Plastic Every Year." *National Geographic*. 5 Jun 2019. *www. nationalgeographic.com/environment/2019/06/you-eat-thousands-of-bits-of-plastic-every-year/#close*. Web. 12 Jan 2020.

76 Norwegian Geotechnical Institute. "When Plastic Is Part of the Food Chain." NGI News. *www.ngi.no/eng/News/ NGI-News/When-plastic-is-part-of-the-food-chain*. Web. 12 Jan 2020.

77 Earth 911. "How to Recycle Plastic Bags." *www.earth911. com/recycling-guide/how-to-recycle-plastic-bags/*. Web. 12 Jan 2020.

78 Rotary. "Guiding Principles." *www.my.rotary.org/en/guid-ing-principles*. Web. 8 Jan 2020.

79 Hayhoe, Katharine. "The Most Important Thing You Can Do to Fight Climate Change: Talk About It." *TEDWomen 2018*. Nov 2018. *www.ted.com/talks/ katharine_hayhoe_the_most_important_thing_you_can_ do_to_fight_climate_change_talk_about_it*.